Keep It Zesty

Keep It Zesty

A Celebration of Lebanese
Flavors & Culture from Edy's Grocer

Edy Massih

HARPER

An Imprint of HarperCollinsPublishers

To my grandfathers, Edouard Hilal & Afif Massih, who have kept Lebanon alive within me.

1 Taste the Rainbow

Dips, Cheeses, Pickles & All the Fixings   35

Contents

KEY:
V = Vegan
VG = Vegetarian
P = Pescatarian
GF = Gluten-free
NF = Nut-free

Contents

KEY:
V = Vegan
VG = Vegetarian
P = Pescatarian
GF = Gluten-free
NF = Nut-free

Hi from Edy's Grocer in Greenpoint, Brooklyn!

I am so excited to bring all our best eats to your kitchen. Whether you have visited us or not, this book will give you the full Edy's Grocer experience, with a rotating menu of Middle Eastern staples, pantry items, and everything you need to host a signature Brown Paper Board spread of your own. Just remember, I'm not your Lebanese grandmother (I'm Edy!), so don't be surprised when you see fresh spins on Middle Eastern classics.

You'll find some of the Grocer's bestsellers, including a spin on my grandmother's perfect Riz a Djej (page 187), my special invention, Pitadillas (page 129), Lebanese staples like Herby Falafel (page 164) and Lahm Bi Ajin Squares (page 174), and a whole chapter of refreshing drinks to wash it all down (page 229). You'll learn to stock your own shelves with all the spices, condiments, and fixings to transform yourself into a zesty chef, like Spicy Tomato Jam (page 50), Hummus with Dukkah (page 36), labneh with Aleppo Chili Crisp (page 78), and Marinated Feta (page 60). And hosting has never been easier with my simple checklist to build a very Instagram-ready Brown Paper Board (page 29). Along the way, I'll pop up to offer helpful tips and advice to guide you, and I've also included a handy guide for recipes throughout the book that are vegetarian, vegan, pescatarian, gluten-free, and nut-free so you can please all your guests.

I've included recipes for a few key staples, like Za'atar Paste (page 73) and tomato sauce (page 180), that are the building blocks for a lot of dishes in this book, but I've included store-bought substitutes when possible to make your life easier in the kitchen. The tahini sauce (page 76) and vinaigrette charts (page 77), plus my guide to pickling (page 65), are there for you to mix and match seasonal ingredients, use what you have on hand right now, or just make what excites you the most. We're going to cover the perfect dishes for any time of day, from breakfast to dessert.

To me, cooking is all about having fun, giving your spice cabinet a workout, and adding something special to every dish. I think making food is a powerful act of love, and throughout the book, you'll find my odes to the women who shaped me into the person I am today, in and out of the kitchen. This book comes straight from my heart, which is where every good meal should come from. So dive in, fold pages, take notes, customize, experiment, make mistakes, and have fun! Gather your family and friends and start cooking, tasting, and eating the Edy's Grocer way. As Oprah would say, don't forget to live your best life. And always keep it zesty!

Sahtein,
Edy Massih

The Story of
Edy's Grocer

From Beirut to Boston

Lebanon, a country that combines the traditional spirit of the Arab world with the Western charm of Beirut, is aptly known as the Paris of the Middle East. I was born and raised in Anfeh, a small Greek Orthodox fishing village about an hour north of Beirut, on the shore of the Mediterranean Sea. It's a place and a culture I lost when I moved to America and never expected to appreciate. But the aromatic food, pristine beaches with shimmering blue water, heart-lifting church services, and carefree laughter of its beautiful, resilient people pull me back home and make me proud to be Lebanese.

Anfeh's population is a little over six thousand people, a small stretch of village under two square miles. The village consists of small family-owned businesses, housewives gossiping over coffee and cigarettes, and the most stunning beaches in Lebanon. Growing up, I was surrounded by food day and night, and my world revolved around what we were eating next. Entertaining was a way of life, and my earliest family memories include cooking, feasting, dancing, and laughing around a big table of food. In Anfeh, we were all about sharing, so everything from mezze to mains to dessert was always served family style.

My paternal grandmother, Odette, was

an elegant and proud Lebanese woman, housewife, and mother of four. I'd follow her around, admiring her gorgeous blown-out hair, shoulder-padded suit jacket, and confident, ladylike walk. Every Sunday, she'd come home from church, change into stretchy clothes, turn the stove on low, and swirl two tablespoons of Najjar coffee grounds in a silver Turkish coffee pot. Then she'd dig into her secret stash of British McVitie's Digestive biscuits, kept in a locked drawer in the dining room. She'd arrange the coffee and cookies on a tray and retreat to the balcony with a cigarette, where she'd gossip with whomever was near—her sister, her daughter, or a neighbor.

During her post-church coffee break, I'd cling to my Teita (grandmother in Arabic) as she implored me to join the other kids on the beach. "I will be right there," she'd say. "Go swim, go play with your friends." But I wouldn't move. Instead, I'd ask her to warm me up some kibbeh balls with her homemade garlic labneh. She'd serve it to me with a smile as I sat on the kitchen counter to watch her bring our meal to life. Once she got cooking, she was tireless and unstoppable.

My love for food grew every summer, as I spent less time in the classroom and more time in the kitchen with Teita. Summer lunches at her beach house were the highlight of my day. There was something special about watching Odette pick parsley leaves for the tabbouleh, with the Mediterranean shimmering in the background. She had a small makeshift kitchen in the house with a countertop gas burner, a sink, and four feet of counter space. My grandfather Afif was the grill master, expertly charring fish from the sea or rows of fragrant skewers. In a four-hour window, I'd watch Odette assemble the standard Sunday menu: threading the meat onto skewers for the grill, double frying the French fries, making hummus from scratch, mincing her homegrown parsley for the tabbouleh, grinding garlic to make toum, and binding the kibbeh, all with one hand! (Her left hand was paralyzed when she was young.) She made every meal like it was her last.

On the other side of my family, there was Jacqueline, or Jacquo, as I would call her. Born in Aleppo, Syria, she was my maternal grandmother, who resided between Beirut and Aleppo with my grandfather Edouard (my namesake), who I called Baba. My Baba owned and ran the Syrian headquarters of Bosch, as my grandmother cooked, hosted, and entertained in the breezy Syrian summer nights. Jacquo would say the Lebanese are lazy because they call mezze a meal. She had lived in Geneva, Switzerland, during the Lebanese war and her way was different. She would thinly slice the potatoes for a gratin, sear a lamb shank and let it braise for hours, but still kept her Syrian heritage by making

kibbeh, a Middle Eastern spiced meatloaf. It was from her that I learned it was possible to combine foods across cultures. She also loved to pickle anything and everything—labneh, cauliflower, stuffed eggplant, turnips. I so vividly remember those tingly, salty, vinegary pickles and the face I would make when biting into them. I could never get enough.

The street food in Aleppo was like nothing I had ever tasted: the cheesy, meaty toshka sandwiches, a tall glass of salted yogurt ayran, or the pistachio and sesame-crusted barazek cookies. The restaurants were always so elegant, and the service was phenomenal. My favorite part was the hot, fluffy bread with the succulent red kibbeh nayyeh, a raw meat tartare, with a side of French fries dipped in toum. Every restaurant had their own version of a muhammara dip, some with breadcrumbs, some with walnuts, with or without pomegranate molasses. The food traditions in Syria were different from those in Lebanon, and the holidays and restrictions varied, but in both countries food and family were the most important things. No matter how busy she was, Jacquo always maintained her traditions, keeping her table and freezer packed with great food.

When it came to hosting, both grandmothers would start planning the menu at least five days ahead and start shopping, prepping, and cooking no less than three days ahead. Cooking was no joke for Jacqueline and Odette—it was their job, and they excelled at it.

Dinners were an especially grand event. The menu was always extensive, starting

My grandfathers,
Edouard & Afif

My grandmothers,
Odette &
Jacqueline

My mom and dad's engagement

My sister, me, and our little cousin Carlos

My summers at the beach in Anfeh

with mezze, bites, and accoutrements. Then it was the main dishes, elegantly plated with an abundance of pine nuts, pistachios, cashews, herbs, and dried flowers. There was always a showstopper that needed the most extensive amount of prep, work, care, and love, with many supporting dishes. The desserts were just as important, and of course prepared ahead. French-inspired cakes like gateau aux marrons, pistachio macarons cake, or orange blossom cake; cookies like ma'amoul or biscuit au chocolat; puddings like rosewater rice pudding, meghli pudding, or creme caramel; all the phyllo delicacies like osmalieh, knafeh, and baklava; and the American-influenced Jell-O layered with fruits and arranged in all sorts of sculptures and molds. Everything on the table had a purpose and there was never repetition. It was all thought out with the right amount of spices, flavors, and textures and more than enough to feed a crowd.

Starting from the age of four, my parents would send my sister, Natacha, and me to visit my cousins in Geneva and attend summer camp. Being in a cosmopolitan city with rich cheeses, hanging sausage and thinly sliced salami, luscious ice cream with chocolate shavings, Nutella-filled crêpes, and the best poulet rôti with fries dipped in mayonnaise was heavenly. Curfew was early in Geneva and they had electricity all day long, so the streets were silent at night. In Lebanon, we only had electricity at certain hours, so the streets were a communal

living room at night with people socializing, eating, drinking, and playing games. The restrained culture of Geneva was a whole new concept to me.

As a family, we couldn't escape the reality that the unrest in the Middle East meant Lebanon was crumbling around us, so in 2004, my parents decided that we would move together to Boston, where my dad had gotten a job. I was only nine then, and it was hard for me to grasp that I was really leaving, and to understand what it would mean to lose my extended family, my culture, my eating habits, my friends, my language, my beach, and my people and move to Massachusetts. But when I look back, my parents sacrificed just as much and more to better our future and life—for that I am grateful.

Unable to speak a word of English, I was scared and isolated. In post-9/11 America, showing up as a Lebanese immigrant in a predominantly white community made me the target of relentless bullying. My parents were busier in Boston than in Anfeh, but my mom insisted on having dinner around the table every night as a family. It was important to sit together, discuss our day, and check in, but because both my parents worked full-time jobs, at ten I started stepping in to help make dinner.

I started off with a small repertoire that included chicken burgers, fettuccine or ravioli, and sometimes shawarma skewers. The burden of being bullied, of being called names, and the pressure to speak unaccented English all dissipated as I'd rolled out Pillsbury pie crust to make my own version of savory mini croissants. I would stuff them with sliced deli ham and cheese from Stop & Shop, top them with sautéed mushrooms, and always finish them off with an egg wash, Jacquo's finishing touch. During the few times that Odette and Jacquo came to visit my family in Boston, they'd share their culinary secrets with me, wanting to keep their traditions alive. Notebook in hand, I learned how to make stuffed potatoes and whole chicken filled with rice and ground lamb, an unforgettable dish. One time Odette yelled at me, "What, are you a lazy American now?" because I'd wanted to use Minute Rice instead of jasmine rice to make her riz a djej. I couldn't help but laugh as I hid the offensive rice from her view.

After what felt like a lifetime, I returned to Lebanon at the age of fourteen to visit my family. It was summertime when I returned to Anfeh, and everything felt so surreal. All the memories I was holding on to came flooding back: the beach, the grilled fish, the French fries, the long trip to Aleppo, that kibbeh nayyeh—except this time I would scarf down two toshkas instead of one. Speaking Arabic and French all day after having to communicate only in English for five years was a wild sensation. While playing cards at night with Odette and Jacqueline, I would try to get more recipes out of them. They kept their secrets guarded, but I would follow them into the kitchen and

watch anyway. It was never easy to leave, but it was always a celebration to go back every summer. I would hold on to the food memories, often salivating thinking about what my first meal would be when I landed back in Beirut.

Middle school was a drag. I attended ESL classes all day, and the bullying continued to be horrendous. Every day, I would race home, grab my Diet Coke and Cheez-Its, and glue myself to the TV at 4 p.m. for the *Oprah Winfrey Show*. As soon as it was over, I would get in the kitchen and make all the things I had been daydreaming about during school.

By the time I reached high school, I was finally speaking fluent English, and my thick accent began to fade away. I started to relax and figure out who I really was. When my high school cut cooking classes from their curriculum for budgetary reasons, I petitioned and started my own after-school cooking club, held in the cafeteria. Students actually showed up, and the cooking club turned into my own broadcast cooking series on the local public access channel, taped from my home kitchen once a week. I knew I wanted to become a chef, that food was my way to find myself and keep Lebanon alive within me. So, after high school, I left Boston to attend the Culinary Institute of America.

Jammal Restaurant in Batroun

Making manoushe in my hometown

Hallab 1881, my grandfather's favorite sweet shop

From Boston to Brooklyn

The Culinary Institute of America (CIA) was located in New York's Hudson Valley, and moving there was anything but easy. When I first came to America, I wasn't alone—though it had felt like it at the time. My family was my support system, even if they were going through the same culture-shock changes that I was.

Going to college was different. I was really on my own and started to learn what my real voice was and who I aspired to be. I started to identify my own values and tried to channel some level of wisdom and grace, even though I had no idea what I was doing.

The CIA housed a diverse mix of students from across the country and around the world. It was a community of foodies from every background, color, creed, and sexual orientation. Up until that point, I'd been brainwashed by society to think being Lebanese was a bad thing, so I grew to hate where I came from. CNN only featured Lebanon in the context of war and terrorist attacks, but never for its rich culture, history, food, or heritage. I had started believing that Lebanon was nothing but a war zone after all.

During my sophomore year of culinary school, I packed up two suitcases and moved to the tiny town of Orvieto in the Umbria region of Italy, working as a cook at a small family-owned restaurant for four months. Walking to work every day reminded me of Anfeh, my home, and I started to feel homesick. The ladies sitting outside on their benches and plastic white chairs gossiping, the church bells, the mini-markets, and all the small businesses—it felt like I had been transported back to my childhood. The Italian pride in their culture was infectious and stirred a pride in me too.

The sous-chef, Carlos, didn't speak English, so I learned to speak a rough version of Italian. It could be difficult to communicate at times, but we shared a common language: our love of cooking. He taught me that sauces and stews needed patience and care, and that it was important to pay attention to every step, putting the right time into mixing, adjusting the heat, and tasting for balance. It reminded me of the amount of pristine attention my grandmothers had spent cooking up the homemade dishes of my childhood. Making something special should take time— the longer something simmers, the more expansive the flavors: it soaks up the love.

That summer, I traveled around Italy— Rome, Siena, Bologna, Venice, Milan, Florence, Modena, to the Tuscan beaches— and found that each region had its own style of cooking, with specialty dishes. Each spoke Italian just a little differently, but no matter where I visited, the grandmothers were always there gossiping on benches. Each town had its own captivating duomo with stained glass, sculptures, paintings, arches, and bells. When I stepped inside each cathedral, I could feel the energy radiating all around me.

I had planned to fly from Rome to Beirut in August when my time in Orvieto was done, but I was exhausted from working all summer and decided to cancel my flight and head back to Boston early. A few days after I returned to the States, Odette passed away after a long battle with cancer. My Teita Odette, who taught me everything I believe in: how to stand in the kitchen all day, how to seamlessly entertain, how to value family, and how to preserve Lebanese food and culture. I was supposed to be there. I was supposed to be with her in her final days. I was heartbroken.

Losing a Lebanese grandmother is heavy on the family. My friend William recently lost his grandmother and said, "The loss of a Lebanese grandmother is like no other—she is who your family gathered round. She is the one who first showed you your favorite dishes. It's her scent and words of wisdom that come to life when you close your eyes." Teita Odette had been battling cancer for years, and I know she is in a better place now and no longer in pain. But I felt like my time with her had been cut short—I still had so much to learn. I hadn't learned how to make her orange cake or samkeh harra or sayadieh. I looked up to her so much, and I always felt like I owed it to her to stay in the closet. She was a true Christian—she fasted every Lent, never ever missed mass on Sunday, attended every celebration, wedding, and funeral—and I worried that her traditional religious views made her less likely to accept my identity. The possibilities of rejection or losing my

relationship with her were too painful to even imagine.

Once she passed, I started to get more comfortable with the idea of coming out. It's never easy, and the first step—and often the hardest one—is coming out to yourself. One day, after class, I went into my dorm room and looked at myself in the mirror. Suddenly, everything I had suppressed for years came flooding back, and I had what felt like an out-of-body experience. I was gay. I knew, at that point, that everything would change, whether I wanted it to or not. I might be treated differently by friends and family, I could even lose loved ones from my life, but I knew then that it was worth it, that there was no going back. I had to be the true me.

Coming out also helped me advocate more for my Lebanese identity. Back at the CIA, I drummed up the courage to meet with the dean to express how I didn't think the Mediterranean Cuisine Class was authentic— half the recipes didn't make any sense to me! I was shocked that instead of valuing my opinion and my heritage, he told me that everything gets Americanized, whether it's Asian, Middle Eastern, Italian, or Mexican— after all, it's called the Culinary Institute of *America* for a reason. That meeting was a huge awakening to me, and I realized the immense responsibility I had to preserve my culinary traditions.

Attending the CIA was my dream, but it felt like the bubble had popped. Everything lost its sheen. A few months later, in a moment of overwhelm, I plagiarized part of

The main Greek Orthodox church in Anfeh

The beach in my hometown

a history paper and my life came crumbling down. I hit my lowest moment. I had just lost Odette, come out of the closet, and now was suspended. How was I going to tell my parents that I had failed? What was I going to do?

The call to my parents, unsurprisingly, did not go well. My parents forced me to make a choice: either I could come back to Boston, live with them, and work at a local restaurant for a year to save money before heading back to college or I could go off on my own.

From Brooklyn to Edy's Grocer

As I'm sure you guessed, I didn't go back home to Boston. A professor helped me land an internship at *Wine & Spirits* magazine and a line cook job at Corkbuzz in Chelsea Market. Freshly twenty years old, I packed two suitcases and moved into a three-bedroom apartment in Williamsburg with total strangers. I was thrown into the real world, but I was ambitious and eager to learn. I was a young sponge, ready to absorb it all.

Living in New York, I was hard-pressed to find Lebanese representation in the food scene, and I became determined to change that. Why weren't there more Lebanese restaurants, like in London, Paris, or Montreal? The only one I could find was Ilili, an upscale restaurant way out of my price range. After dabbling around with freelance catering work, in 2016 I decided to take the big step of starting my own catering company.

I began with small opportunities, like office catering, private rooftop events, and cocktail parties. Even though I was young, I was hungry to please, willing to bend over backward to sign an event, make a

dollar, and learn. Word of mouth grew, and eventually I was catering breakfast and lunch for companies such as Victoria's Secret, Uniqlo, and Spotify. It was a thrill watching the events come to life, and business was booming, but the work and stress took a toll on my body, which is when I started to shed my hair.

Learning to set boundaries for myself was hard, especially when I was eager to say yes to everything. It was a process, but eventually I started taking advantage of the slow winter season to give myself the gift of travel. From South Africa to Bali to Australia, I was able to absorb, learn, taste, and grow. Unsurprisingly, I found that giving myself time off and allowing myself to say no to things actually made me better at my job. Taking time off from constant work also allowed me to learn who I truly was, and through therapy and lots of journaling, I was able to find my true values in life: community, authenticity, connection, pleasure, creativity, and zest.

After finding my groove with catering, in the summer of 2018 I took another big step: I reached out to my community and started my Farm to Table backyard dinner series. With the help and motivation of my friend the talented chef James Park, I started hosting biweekly dinners in my Greenpoint backyard with twenty-six seats that sold out in hours. I loved bringing a crowd together, and people came from every borough in the city (and even Connecticut and New Jersey!) to share a meal inspired by the Lebanese cooking that I grew up with. The food turned strangers into friends, and these dinners helped me solidify my professional identity. In February 2020, I left for a vacation to Australia and by the time I returned to New York on March 13, 2020, everything imploded.

One week into the pandemic, after shutting down my catering career and returning all the deposits to my clients, I felt like I was going crazy. I was itching to cook, to express myself through my food, but every path kept leading to a dead end. Plus, I had lost my entire source of income. I was almost out of ideas, but not quite.

I had lived around the corner from Maria's Deli in Greenpoint for three years. I often stopped by for deli sandwiches or just popped in to say hello to Maria Puk, a Polish immigrant who had moved to Greenpoint from Poland at the age of seven. She used to hang out at the deli when it was a grocery store owned by her neighbor Nick Hanuszczak. From age eleven to fifteen, Maria worked at Nick's grocery store, and in 1978, Maria and her sister, Teresa, purchased the

building and the store became Maria's Deli. (She was twenty-five when she took over the building, and forty-three years later she passed it to me not long after my twenty-fifth birthday.) Under Maria's ownership, it became a neighborhood staple, and she ran the deli for forty-three years. She reminded me of my Teita Odette, with her warm smile and welcoming presence. Far from my family—both in Boston and in Lebanon—Maria's Deli became a home away from home.

Over the years, Maria and I had a running joke that one day the corner deli would become mine, so I needed to start saving up! The talk never seemed serious until the summer of 2020, when I got a call from Maria. She said she had spoken to her family, and she was ready to retire. All of a sudden, things were about to change, fast.

I put together a business plan and started thinking about what type of shop I wanted to open. I knew that I wanted to have a wide variety of homemade mezze, breakfast, lunch, and dinner items. I wanted customers to be able to drop in and pick up all their needs for their dinner party or discover something special to spice up their meals. Then it struck me—through my years of catering out of my apartment in Greenpoint, I had always bemoaned the lack of a Middle Eastern market near me. I would have to trek to Sahadi's or Kalustyan's, and I always wished I could just dash somewhere in Greenpoint when I needed pomegranate molasses or sumac in a pinch. Finally, I knew exactly what the Grocer would be.

Me at the CIA

With Maria and
her husband, John,
on signing day

With John, Maria, my mom,
sister, and dad on opening day

Maria and I did a walk-through of the store. The kitchen was smaller than I expected, with no walk-in refrigerator, and the unfinished basement was full of forty-three years of clutter. Upstairs, Teresa lit a cigarette in the middle of the kitchen as she sipped her coffee and told me there was no room for negotiation—I would need to take it as is. They ran through the key fee, the monthly lease, the water bill, the building taxes, and the electricity. I told them that I needed free rent until I opened, but they would only agree to six weeks. By July 1 we had signed the contract and the construction began.

As a twenty-five-year-old, I had no idea what I was doing. But while the city was dead, and everything was closing, I had so much help. Friends came by to move things, make Home Depot runs, deep-clean oily shelves, and shove ovens into place. The community I had built—that I had fed for years—was showing up for me. After coming to New York five years before, knowing nobody, it was a beautiful moment to see everything come together.

I reached out to Sahadi's and Baroody—the two biggest Middle Eastern importers in the area—and started picking out items from their catalogs. My vision was to stock my freshly painted pink and green shelves full of the Middle Eastern staples and grocery items that I could never find in my neighborhood. I started writing the menu—heavily inspired by my catering days—filled with Lebanese classics with the creative twists that had become my specialty. I started building my team and planning a coffee program for my newly installed takeout window on the side of the building. But, right as everything was falling into place, the worst thing imaginable happened: the August 4, 2020, explosion in Beirut.

I saw the headline alert on my phone the morning our first big order was arriving to the store. The store had consumed my life, but my loved ones were more important—I dropped everything to get in contact with my family and make sure they were safe. Thankfully, everyone was okay, and as my heart rate began to slow, I turned to the news, slowly understanding the enormous aftermath of the explosion, which, to me, seemed bigger than Hiroshima and destroyed the city that I loved and cherished.

It was less than a year since I had last visited Beirut, and the city was demolished. Every store, every restaurant, every block. I watched in horror and awe as the poor citizens of Beirut picked up the debris and swept up the city with no help from the government. As I went through the motions of unpacking boxes—something I had looked forward to for months—I cried, watching videos of stores, malls, gas stations, restaurants, and homes in the aftermath of the explosion. My friends sent me videos of their homes, completely destroyed. I didn't know how to react or respond. It was an attack on my people, and suddenly the store and everything I worked so hard to build felt irrelevant. My mind was in Beirut, but, back in Brooklyn, I was eight days away from opening.

Beirut survived because of an outpouring of love from around the world and the resilience of the people. This devastating moment solidified my purpose: I would open this store and make my people proud; I would spread the love and joy of Lebanese culture and food. I chose August 15 for our opening—my grandmother's favorite holiday, Eid el Saydeh, the Virgin Mary's birthday. In Anfeh, it was a day that everyone came together at the beach for a night of prayer, feasting, fireworks, and swimming. Odette passed away two days after her favorite holiday, so it felt like the best way to honor my Teita, whom I missed so much. I hung her photo over the entrance to the kitchen, so she could always be with me in the kitchen.

The day Edy's Grocer opened, we sold out of every mezze, cheese, breakfast, and main on offer. I was surrounded (masked and socially distanced, don't worry!) by neighbors, family, loved ones, industry friends, and the Instagram community that had watched me transform the deli into my dream space. It filled my heart that they were all there to experience that happy moment with me.

Fast forward to today. I'm still juggling a (thankfully!) thriving business, popping up on the *Forbes* 30 Under 30 list, cooking with Drew Barrymore, bartending for Andy Cohen, and reinventing my catering business that is bigger and better than ever. Oh, and writing this book!

In everything I do, I keep it zesty. It's been a long road with a lot of ups and downs, but in every project, collaboration, and event, I carry with me the values that I've worked so hard to build. Everything I do is inspired by who I am, where I came from, and what I stand for. I'm proud to be Lebanese, I'm proud to be gay, I'm proud to be a chef, and I'm beyond proud to bring my communities together in a space that's safe and welcoming to all.

I'm still learning and growing every day, but what I know for sure is that the power of food and cooking brings a deeper awareness, connection, and expression of the person I've always been. The most rewarding part of this whole journey—from Beirut to Boston to Brooklyn—has been being able to keep my traditions alive, keep my family in my heart, and bring a whole new audience closer to my culture.

Pink & Green Shelves
How to Stock a Zesty Kitchen

The Middle Eastern Pantry

In Middle Eastern countries, pantry items are sold in large markets and tiny storefronts, with each vendor specializing in a few items. The aromas of fresh spices, the sounds of bargaining, the feeling of grains running through your fingers are all part of the shopping experience. At the Grocer we work with importers to source the best versions of everything on our shelves.

To build your own home pantry, I urge you to explore your local grocery store, where the quality of Middle Eastern ingredients continues to improve every day. There might even be a Middle Eastern store or specialty spice shop near you! And if all else fails, two of my favorite New York institutions—Kalustyan's and Sahadi's—ship nationally. (Edy's Grocer also ships nationally from edysgrocer.com.) These are the base spices used for every dish in this book, but they're also great to just have in your pantry for experimenting and everyday use. Here's everything you'll need to keep it zesty!

Spices

Aleppo Pepper: A type of chile pepper that originated in Syria. It has a moderately spicy flavor with a fruity, slightly sweet undertone—like a milder and more flavorful version of crushed red pepper flakes.
Put it to use: Spicy Fig Jam (page 54), Aleppo Chili Crisp (page 78), Aleppo Garlic Shrimp Cocktail (page 173).

Baharat: A spice blend that typically includes some combination of black pepper, cumin, coriander, cinnamon, and cloves, as well as other spices like nutmeg, cardamom, and paprika. It has a warm, complex taste and is used heavily in cooking.
Put it to use: Aajeh, Lebanese Frittata (page 102); Chickpea & Eggplant Stew (page 181); Riz a Djej (page 187)

Baharat
Add 2 tablespoons ground allspice, 2 tablespoons freshly ground black pepper, 2 tablespoons ground coriander, 1 tablespoon ground cinnamon, 1 tablespoon ground cloves, 1 tablespoon ground nutmeg, and ½ tablespoon ground cardamom to a small jar. Seal and shake the jar to combine all the ingredients thoroughly. Store in a cool, dry place for up to 6 months. Makes ¾ cup baharat.

Shawarma Seasoning

Add 2 tablespoons smoked paprika, 2 tablespoons dried parsley, 1 tablespoon dried oregano, 1 tablespoon ground cumin, 1 tablespoon onion powder, 1 tablespoon garlic powder, 1 tablespoon kosher salt, and 1 teaspoon freshly ground black pepper to a small jar. Seal and shake the jar to combine all the ingredients thoroughly. Store in a cool, dry place for up to 6 months. Makes ½ cup shawarma seasoning.

Put it to use: Chicken Shawarma Wrap (page 132), Shawarma Chicken Taco Night (page 166), Shawarma Chicken Fatteh (page 200)

Dukkah

Heat 3 tablespoons vegetable oil in a small skillet over medium heat. Add 1 cup pumpkin seeds and fry, stirring occasionally, until just starting to brown, about 5 minutes. Use a slotted spoon to remove the pumpkin seeds to a medium jar. Add 1 cup sesame seeds to the skillet and stir often until lightly golden and fragrant, about 2 minutes. Transfer the sesame seeds to the jar with the pumpkin seeds, along with ½ cup za'atar and ½ cup sumac. Seal and shake the jar to combine all the ingredients thoroughly. Store in a cool, dry place for up to 6 months. Makes 3 cups dukkah.

Put it to use: Hummus with Dukkah (page 36), Dukkah Pita Chips (page 108), Kale Tabbouleh (page 117)

Cumin: Cumin is commonly used in both ground and whole seed form. It has a warm, earthy flavor and is the base flavor of a lot of rice, meat, and vegetable dishes. I use ground cumin in my shawarma seasoning.
Put it to use: Charred Baba Ganoush (page 53), Cumin, Carrot & Coconut Soup (page 123), Garlicky Potato Salad (page 160)

Dried Herbs: Dried herbs are more concentrated in flavor than fresh herbs, and sometimes even take on a slightly different flavor. Lebanese cooking leans heavily on dried herbs, especially dried mint, dried oregano, and dried parsley.
Put them to use: Beiruti Balila (page 66), Marinated Olives (page 67), Kibbeh Bi Laban (page 194)

Rose Petals: Dried rose petals are a potent, fragrant, and colorful touch, used in teas, desserts, and sometimes even savory meat and rice dishes, where they add a surprisingly delicate touch. Make sure to source edible flowers that are chemical-free.
Put them to use: Orange Blossom Osmalieh (page 218), Rosewater Spritz (page 235)

Sumac: A tart, lemony spice used in Middle Eastern cooking. It's made by grinding the dried berries of the sumac plant into a dark, wine-colored powder. It is a common ingredient used to add a tangy flavor to meats, dips, salads, and dressings.
Put it to use: Spatchcock Sumac Chicken (page 169), Everything Sumac Salmon (page 146), Spicy Sumac Margarita (page 235)

Za'atar: A spice blend that typically includes a combination of dried thyme, oregano or marjoram, and sumac and sesame seeds. Each country, region, and vendor has its own delicious blend with a signature tangy, herbal, slightly sour flavor.

Put it to use: Za'atar Manoushe (page 89), Za'atar Shakshuka (page 98), Za'atar Chicken Thighs (page 145)

Seeds & Grains

Basmati and Jasmine Rice: Both are fragrant types of long-grain rice, but basmati has a nutty flavor and fluffy texture while jasmine has a delicate floral aroma and a slightly sticky texture. Basmati is better for dishes where the rice should be separated and light; jasmine can be used where the rice can be a little denser.

Couscous: A type of pasta made from semolina flour; I lean toward the larger pearl couscous. It has a light, fluffy texture that is a perfect base for salads, an addition to soups, or as a side dish for meat and vegetable dishes.

Lentils: Small, disk-shaped legumes that come in a variety of colors, including brown, green, and red. Green is the most commonly used in Lebanon, perfect for boosting soups, salads, and rice dishes.

Za'atar

To make your own za'atar blend, toast 2 tablespoons sesame seeds in a small skillet over medium heat for about 2 minutes, until they're lightly golden and fragrant. Transfer to a jar to cool. In a spice grinder, pulse 2 tablespoons dried thyme, 1 tablespoon dried oregano, and 2 teaspoons dried mint until finely crushed. Add to the jar with the sesame seeds, along with 2 tablespoons sumac and 1 teaspoon kosher salt. Seal and shake the jar to combine all the ingredients thoroughly. Store in a cool, dry place for up to 6 months. Makes 1 cup za'atar.

Herby Harissa Seasoning

Add ¼ cup Aleppo pepper, 2 tablespoons dried parsley, 2 tablespoons dried oregano, 2 tablespoons dried mint, 2 tablespoons dried thyme, and 1 tablespoon kosher salt to a small jar. Seal and shake the jar to combine all the ingredients thoroughly. Store in a cool, dry place for up to 6 months. Makes 1 cup herby harissa.

Put it to use: Sizzling Sun-Dried Tomatoes (page 65), Harissa Lime Brussels Sprouts (page 150)

Edy's Everything Seasoning

Add ½ cup store-bought everything bagel seasoning, 2 tablespoons Aleppo pepper, 1 tablespoon nigella seeds, 1 tablespoon fennel seeds, and 1 tablespoon cumin seeds to a small jar. Seal and shake the jar to combine all the ingredients thoroughly. Store in a cool, dry place for up to 6 months. Makes ¾ cup everything seasoning.

Put it to use: Everything Salmon Salad (page 52), Fast Croissants (page 94), BEC Everything Empanadas (page 105), Everything Sumac Salmon (page 146), Shrimp Fatteh (page 200)

I strongly believe every cook should stock kosher salt and only kosher salt. Here's why:

1. Easy to handle: Kosher salt has larger grains than table salt, which makes it easier to pick up and sprinkle with your fingers.
2. Enhanced flavor: Kosher salt has a less intense flavor than table salt and does not contain iodine or any other additives. This means that it allows the natural flavors of the food to shine through and doesn't overwhelm the dish with saltiness.
3. Better texture: The larger grains of kosher salt dissolve more slowly than table salt, which can help distribute the salt more evenly and provide a better texture to meat, fish, and vegetables.
4. Consistent quality: Kosher salt is produced according to strict standards, which ensures that it has a consistent texture and flavor from batch to batch.

I used Diamond Crystal kosher salt in developing all the recipes in this book. If using Morton's, halve the amount and taste to adjust.

Nigella Seeds: Small, black seeds that have a slightly bitter, peppery flavor. They're traditionally used to season breads, pickles, and falafel, and I like to use them as a perfect twist to the popular everything seasoning.

Orzo: A type of pasta that is shaped like a grain of rice. Just like its cousin couscous, it's perfect as a side dish or added to soups and salads.

Sesame Seeds: Tiny, white seeds heavily used in Middle Eastern cuisine. They have a nutty flavor and a slightly crunchy texture and are used as a garnish for bread, pastries, and falafel or as a seasoning for salads, meats, and vegetables.

Staples

Kosher Salt: Kosher salt has a large grain for easy and accurate seasoning, plus a pleasing flavor that enhances everything from savory to sweet dishes.

Date Molasses: Date molasses, also known as date syrup, is a sweet syrup made from cooked and mashed dates. It has a deep, caramel-like flavor and is often used as a sweetener or a condiment.

Greek Yogurt: Greek yogurt is a thick and creamy yogurt made by straining regular yogurt for a richer and more concentrated product. With a tangy taste and a velvety texture, it's a versatile ingredient for dips, sauces, marinades, and desserts. It's also an easy and healthy substitute for sour cream, cream cheese, and mayonnaise.

Harissa Paste: A spicy paste made from chile peppers, garlic, and other seasonings. It is commonly used to add deep flavor and a punch of heat to meat and vegetable dishes.

Lemons: Lemons are perfect for their tangy and acidic flavor in a variety of dishes, from savory to sweet. Lemon juice boosts marinades, dressings, and sauces, while the zest can be used to add a bright and fresh flavor to everything from rich meats to baked goods.

Orange Blossom Water: Made by steeping white orange blossoms in water, giving it a sweet, citrusy flavor. Similar to rosewater, it's used to add an intriguing flavor to desserts and drinks.

Tahini: A paste made from ground sesame seeds that is one of the most commonly used ingredients in Middle Eastern cuisine. It has a nutty flavor and a creamy texture, and most often is added to dips and sauces.

Edy's Tip

Make Greek yogurt your best friend! I always keep a container of fat-free Greek yogurt on hand, and here's why:

1. It's healthy: High in protein, low in fat, and packed with calcium, it's just a better choice when a recipe uses dairy. I stick to fat-free yogurt so my dishes are rich without feeling overly heavy.
2. It's versatile: It can be used in a variety of dishes, from savory dips and sauces to sweet desserts, and can be flavored with herbs, spices, or fruit to create a wide range of flavor profiles.
3. It's alive: Greek yogurt contains live and active cultures, which are beneficial for gut health. These cultures can help improve digestion and overall health.

At the Grocer, we buy lemons in bulk and set aside time to squeeze the juice all at once. A little extra effort now means plenty of fresh lemon juice at the ready later. Just turn on your favorite playlist, grab a pint jar or leftover takeout container, fill it up with freshly squeezed juice, label it with the date, and use it within 4 to 5 days of squeezing.

Pomegranate Molasses: A sweet-tart syrup made from pomegranate juice that has been reduced to a thick consistency. It is a common ingredient used to add flavor to salads, meat dishes, and dips.

Preserved Lemons: Lemons that have been pickled in salt and lemon juice. They have a tart, salty flavor and are commonly used to add flavor to stews, tagines, and salads.

Rosewater: Rosewater is made by steeping rose petals in water, giving it a sweet, floral flavor. It's most often used in desserts and drinks. Just remember, a little goes a long way.

Turkish Coffee: Turkish coffee is made by a method of brewing finely ground coffee beans in a pot with water and sugar. It is a strong, aromatic coffee, traditionally served unfiltered, and enjoyed after a meal as a digestif or as part of a social gathering with sweets.

Very Good Olive Oil: Good-quality olive oil is worth its weight in gold. It'll add extraordinary flavor to salads, dips, soups, and roasts. Look for a cold-pressed extra-virgin olive oil that has a rich, fruity flavor with a peppery finish. Saifan, a Lebanese brand, is my favorite.

Tools of the Trade

A successful kitchen isn't just a stocked pantry. Having the right tool at the right time will make your life easier, your cooking more enjoyable, and your dishes more precise. These are all my favorite tools to have on hand.

Baking Sheets: Rimmed baking sheets, also known as half sheet pans, are the standard vessel for the oven, but can also be used to organize ingredients, drain fried foods, or freeze baked goods.

Blender: A blender is key for silky smooth soups, mixed drinks, cohesive sauces, and perfectly emulsified dressings.

Cheesecloth: A lightweight, woven fabric used for draining liquids, straining yogurt, or making cheese. Hand wash and dry thoroughly to reuse it several times.

Cutting Board: A large, sturdy cutting board made of wood, plastic, or bamboo helps protect your counters, keeps your knives in shape, and provides a sanitary space for slicing and dicing.

Food Processor: My food processor is my go-to for making sauces, dips, or even just chopping lots of herbs.

Garlic Slicer: A garlic slicer (I like the one by OXO) is faster and more efficient than slicing with a knife and guarantees perfectly even pieces.

Knife: A chef's knife is the most essential kitchen tool. Find one that is at a comfortable price point and comfortable size. Most injuries happen with a dull knife, so keep it nice and sharp for precision and safe use.

Lemon Juicer: A handheld tool to squeeze the juice from citrus fruits like lemons and limes. At the Grocer we use an elecrtic juicer, which is faster and more efficient than squeezing them by hand.

Mixing Bowls: Buy a set in various sizes—plastic, glass, or stainless steel are all good—for mixing, marinating, tossing, or serving.

Parchment Paper: Parchment paper helps prevent food from sticking to surfaces and makes cleanup easier. Bleached and unbleached paper are interchangeable.

Pots and Pans: Buy a set in small, medium, and large sizes—stainless steel or nonstick—for boiling, sautéing, frying, searing, and simmering.

Spatula: A silicone spatula is essential for folding, scraping, and spreading food. I have a large one for most jobs and a small one to reach tight places, like the bottom of a jar.

Edy's Tip

I always use parchment paper, never aluminum foil, for a few simple reasons:

1. Nonstick surface: Parchment paper is designed to be a nonstick surface, which means your food is less likely to cling on compared to aluminum foil. This makes it a great choice for baking delicate or sticky food.
2. Eco-friendly: Parchment paper is biodegradable and compostable, which means it is a more environmentally friendly option than aluminum foil. Aluminum foil is not biodegradable and can take up to four hundred years to break down in a landfill.
3. Food safety: Parchment paper is made from natural materials and does not contain any harmful chemicals or coatings, which means it is a safer option for cooking and wrapping food than aluminum foil.

Edy's Tip

Both of my grandmothers stocked a freezer like it was their job. It's a trait I have inherited and a practice I stand by. Here's why you should load up your freezer:

1. Convenience: When you have homemade meals and snacks stocked in your freezer, you always have something quick and easy to eat. This can be a lifesaver on busy weeknights, when company is coming, or when you're sick of cooking. I also like to make big batches of bases like tomato sauce (page 180) or chickpeas (page 38) so I have solid building blocks ready to go.
2. Money: Buy ingredients in bulk and take advantage of sales, saving the extras for later. Or double a recipe, using all the same ingredients, for one meal right now and one in the freezer for later.
3. Waste: Food lasts longer in the freezer than the fridge or pantry. Freezing leftovers gives them a longer life or rescues any ingredients that might go bad before you have a chance to use them. I also freeze extra produce at peak freshness for an unexpected treat months from now, or scraps of vegetables and herbs to make stock later.
4. Health: When you make your own food, you have control over the ingredients and can choose healthier options like whole grains, fresh produce, and lean proteins. You'll be able to dodge all the preservatives in packaged food while enjoying the convenience of ready-to-go meals.

Spice Grinder: My spice grinder never leaves my counter! I use it to grind whole spices, like cumin or peppercorns, but it's also great for making fresh spice blends.

Storage Containers: Storage containers in plastic, glass, or metal keep leftovers fresh, food prep organized, and make for easy meals on the go.

Wooden Spoon: A wooden spoon is the universal kitchen tool, perfect for stirring, mixing, and scooping food and especially handy to keep nonstick pans safe.

Zester: A zester, or a rasp grater, pulls the colorful and aromatic zest from citrus fruits like lemons, limes, and oranges and it's also ideal for grating garlic. You can't keep it zesty without a zester!

How to Build a
Brown Paper Board™

My signature Brown Paper Board, like most great ideas, happened by accident. During my first year of catering, I arrived at a photo shoot set and realized I forgot some of my platters back at the kitchen. Someone on set had already laid brown butcher paper on my table and my friend Ross McCallum, who was a stylist on the shoot, suggested arranging the food directly on the clean paper. I made a beautiful spread and grabbed a Sharpie to label it all. From that point on, I started trading in my platters for bulk rolls of brown paper. I've always believed food should be fun, accessible, and communal, so one board at a time my creativity grew! Here is everything you need to know to make your next gathering extra zesty.

Why build a Brown Paper Board? I'm glad you asked!

It's a visual centerpiece to feast on with your eyes. With a simple piece of brown butcher paper, you can transform your boring table into a feast. You don't need other table accessories, like vases or candles, to make your table look beautiful. Let the vibrant spread speak for itself. Using fresh, seasonal produce will add a pop of color, and edible flowers, herbs, and spices are the perfect garnish to dress up your table to make the board feel extra fancy.

It's easily customizable. You can cater to everyone's dietary restrictions. Vegan? Gluten-free? Not a problem. As you're confirming your guest list, remember to ask for any dietary restrictions so you can include a little something for everyone. There is so much room for creativity. It doesn't have to be limited to appetizers or cheese and charcuterie. You can make a board with meats, salads, bites, baked goods, mezze, pickles, and more. Fill up the board with affordable ingredients like baby carrots, radishes, lettuce, and celery to make entertaining on a budget easy. You can also put an entire meal on the table from an appetizer to dessert by dividing your board. (Let your guests decide if they want cake before dinner. It's a party!) And, most importantly, your guests can enjoy the food leisurely at their own pace—even the friend who's always late.

The setup and cleanup couldn't be easier. Casual is the name of the game. It's up to you what goes on a platter and what goes directly on the board. Use your finest china and silverware or serve on store-bought options (just try to be eco-friendly!). Buy a large, cheap roll of brown butcher paper from your local craft store and use a marker to label each dish (and any dietary info) directly on the paper. Get all your prep work out of the way ahead of time so the board is already set up and ready to go by the time the first guest arrives. Instead of running back and forth to the kitchen, you can pour yourself a drink and enjoy the party. And after everyone leaves, cleanup is as simple as folding up the paper and tossing it. It really couldn't be easier!

Building the Board

The best part of building the board is that it looks abundant and impressive, but it's actually so simple to execute. I'll walk you through the process one step at a time and then guide you through a few sample boards to get your creative juices flowing!

Step 1: Cut your brown paper

Begin with a clean, sturdy surface. Carefully cut a piece of brown butcher paper to cover the entire surface. Tape the edges down under the surface to keep it firmly in place.

Step 2: Plate

Place your mezze in separate bowls. I love a wide, shallow bowl for easy dipping. Level up your board by adding some larger dishes like meats, salads, or even dessert bites. Have fun with different colors, shapes, and sizes to add texture.

Step 3: Arrange

Arrange your bowls and plates across the paper, making sure there's plenty of space between them. This sets the base for the rest of the board.

Step 4: Fill it up

The most fun part! Watch your spread come to life as you fill the space between the dishes with colorful crudités, breads, crackers, small bites, and flatbreads directly on the paper.

Step 5: Garnish

Complete your board by sprinkling herbs, spices, and seeds across your mezze.

Step 6: Dig in!

I know that was a lot of work, so take a moment of gratitude to look at the beauty that you just made, snap a pic, maybe tag @edysgrocer, and make sure to enjoy with your loved ones. Yalla, sahtein to you all!

Let's Plan a
Menu

Portion Guides

As a caterer, everyone is always asking me how I know
how much to make for a crowd. Luckily for you, I've included a few of
my easy-to-follow formulas and go-to sample menus below, which will
make planning your next zesty gathering quick, easy, and delicious.

Intimate Gathering
(4 TO 8 PEOPLE)

Bread & crudités
3 to 4 dips
1 to 2 appetizers
1 main
1 salad or grain
1 dessert
1 drink

Zesty Gathering
(8 TO 15 PEOPLE)

Bread & crudités
4 to 6 dips
2 appetizers
2 mains
1 salad or grain
1 to 2 desserts
1 drink

It's a Party!
(16+ PEOPLE)

Bread & crudités
6 to 8 dips
2 to 3 appetizers
2 to 3 mains
1 to 2 salads or grains
2 desserts
1 to 2 drinks

Intimate Gathering
(4 TO 8 PEOPLE)

Yalla, Come Over Dinner Party

Bread & crudités	
Minty Tzatziki	39
Nutty Muhammara	40
Marinated Olives	67
Tomato Halloumi Skillet	101
Za'atar Chicken Thighs	145
Tahini Caesar Salad	114
Any Labneh Mousse	215
Spicy Sumac Margarita	235

Mediterranean Thanksgiving

Bread & crudités	
Orangey Date Carrot Dip	49
Turmeric Cauliflower	46
Any Homemade Ricotta	58
Pickled Beets	71
Cumin, Carrot & Coconut Soup	123
Spicy Fig & Pistachio Stuffins	161
Spatchcock Sumac Chicken	169
Orzo Mac & Cheese	163
Fig & Sesame Ricotta Cake	226
Pomegranate Moscow Mule	233

Zesty Gathering
(8 TO 15 PEOPLE)

A Greenpoint Picnic

Bread & crudités

Hummus with Dukkah	36
Za'atar Goat Cheese	64
Pesto White Bean Dip	44
Marinated Feta	60
Fava Smash	44
Spicy Tomato Jam	54
Aleppo Garlic Shrimp Cocktail	173
Herby Falafel	164
Any Fatteh	197
Za'atar Chicken Salad Sandwich	125
Watermelon Salad	112
Salted Tahini Brownie	213
Salty Chocolate Tahini Cookie	204
Jallab Rosey Iced Tea	234

Brunch Is the New Dinner

Bread & crudités

Any Homemade Ricotta	58
Everything Salmon Salad	52
Garlicky Labneh	55
Green Angel	43
Any Fast Croissants	94
Any Manoushe	89
Za'atar Shakshuka	98
BEC Everything Empanadas	105
Summery Fattoush Salad	108
Biscuit au Chocolat	210
Edy's Cold Brew	86

It's a Party!
(16+ PEOPLE)

Zesty Holiday Party

Bread & crudités

Spicy Fig Jam	54
Sizzling Sun-Dried Tomatoes	65
Marinated Labneh Balls	56
Baked Mediterranean Feta	63
Marinated Shankleesh	61
Beiruti Balila	66
Harissa Lime Brussels Sprouts	150
Any Kibbeh	191
Riz a Djej	187
Papillote Mediterranean Branzino	170
Butternut Squash Kale Salad	113
Pistachio Halva Rice Krispy	207
Orange Blossom Osmalieh	218
Rosewater Spritz	235

Lemony Cocktail Party

Bread & crudités

Hummus with Dukkah	36
Charred Baba Ganoush	53
Green Angel	43
Pesto White Bean Dip	44
Za'atar Goat Cheese	64
Everything Salmon Salad	52
Pickled Jardiniere	72
Herby Falafel	164
Aleppo Garlic Shrimp Cocktail	173
Lahm Bi Ajin Squares	174
Kale Tabbouleh	117
Turkish Coffee Tiramisu	221
Lemony Rosewater Cake	225
Any Lemonade	230
Arak Dirty Martini	237

1

Taste the Rainbow

**Dips, Cheeses,
Pickles &
All the Fixings**

Let's Get Dipping

Hummus with Dukkah

(V, GF, NF)

I've always been fascinated by a chickpea's journey (nerd alert, I know!). I think it's so cool how a dry chickpea expands while soaking, then swells while cooking, then can transform into so many things. At the Grocer, I'm the only one allowed to make the hummus. I soak my chickpeas for two days, just like my grandmothers taught me, and then carefully cook and blend to a perfectly creamy consistency. It's a little extra effort, but I really think fresh chickpeas make the smoothest hummus. When I moved to the US in 2004, I was shocked that people in Boston didn't even know what hummus was. In Lebanon it's our ketchup, always on the table and used on everything. But it caught on so quickly and within a few years it seemed like everyone suddenly had hummus in their fridge. It's the number one seller in the Grocer because it's a perfect basic canvas for everything. I like to serve it with a generous sprinkle of dukkah, but there really are no wrong answers.

Makes 4 cups

1 cup tahini

½ cup fresh lemon juice

4 to 5 garlic cloves, peeled

½ tablespoon kosher salt

½ tablespoon ground cumin

6 cups Cooked Chickpeas (page 38), or 3 (15.5-ounce) cans chickpeas, drained and rinsed

2 tablespoons extra-virgin olive oil

3 tablespoons Dukkah (page 22; optional)

Add the tahini, lemon juice, garlic, salt, cumin, and 1 cup cold water to a food processor. Process for about 30 seconds, until everything is incorporated. Add the chickpeas and process for about 3 minutes, stopping to scrape the sides as needed, until the hummus is smooth. With the processor running, drizzle in the olive oil. Taste for seasoning, adding more water, lemon juice, or salt as needed for a thick, creamy, and well-seasoned hummus. Transfer to a serving bowl. Serve immediately, topped with the dukkah, or transfer to an airtight container and refrigerate for up to 3 days. Top with the dukkah just before serving.

Cooked Chickpeas

Baking soda helps break down chickpeas and gets them to cook more evenly, while bay leaves add a subtle floral accent to balance out the strong bean flavor.

Makes 12 cups

4 cups dried chickpeas
1 tablespoon baking soda
4 bay leaves

1. **Two days before cooking**, add the chickpeas and ½ tablespoon of the baking soda to a large bowl filled with cold water. Cover with plastic wrap. Check the water periodically to make sure the chickpeas are submerged. On the day of cooking, drain and rinse the chickpeas thoroughly.

2. Add the soaked chickpeas and remaining ½ tablespoon baking soda to a large pot. Set over high heat and stir continuously until the baking soda fizzes. Immediately add enough water to cover by 3 inches, along with the bay leaves. Bring to a simmer, then reduce the heat to medium-low. Simmer for 60 to 75 minutes, occasionally skimming the top, adding water as needed, and monitoring the pot to avoid boiling over.

3. To check for doneness, scoop out a few chickpeas and run under cold water. Press between two fingers to make sure they pierce easily and are cooked through—you should be able to easily smush them, but they should still maintain a bit of firmness. Drain the chickpeas and spread them on a rimmed baking sheet to cool. Pack into airtight containers and refrigerate for up to 1 week.

Edy's Tip

Chickpeas can be frozen in airtight containers for up to 3 months. Thaw overnight in the refrigerator before using.

Minty Tzatziki

VG, GF, NF

Labneh is the Middle East's version of Greek-style yogurt. While we in the US use mayonnaise or sour cream as a base for so many things, I grew up with yogurt in everything. Dried mint is also a huge part of Lebanese cooking, and this recipe is inspired by a very minty tzatziki Teita Odette always made. I love the flavor it adds and the fact that it's endlessly customizable—really any fresh or dried herbs would be very welcome here!

Add the yogurt, cucumber, garlic, olive oil, lemon juice, mint, and salt to a large bowl. Mix well to combine. Taste for seasoning. Transfer to a bowl and serve immediately, or transfer to an airtight container and refrigerate for up to 3 days.

Makes 4 cups

1 (32-ounce) container plain fat-free Greek yogurt

1 English cucumber, seeded and diced (about 1 cup)

3 garlic cloves, grated

3 tablespoons extra-virgin olive oil

3 tablespoons fresh lemon juice

1 tablespoon finely chopped fresh mint or 1 teaspoon dried mint

1 tablespoon kosher salt

Nutty Muhammara

V, GF

Muhammara is a popular recipe in Lebanon, Armenia, Turkey, and Syria, and each local region makes it a little bit differently. This recipe is an adaptation of all the versions I've tried from Damascus to Istanbul. Some versions use breadcrumbs, but I like to use walnuts to make it gluten-free. (Swap in pepitas if you have a nut allergy!) One of my favorite ways to use leftover muhammara is to spread it on toast with a fried egg on top or served alongside grilled chicken.

Makes 2½ cups

1 (10-ounce) jar roasted red peppers, drained, or 3 roasted red bell peppers, peeled and seeded

¼ cup fresh lemon juice

3 garlic cloves

1 tablespoon ground cumin

1 tablespoon kosher salt

2 cups walnuts

½ tablespoon pomegranate molasses

Add the peppers, lemon juice, garlic, cumin, salt, and walnuts to a food processor. Process for about 1 minute, until combined. With the processor running, drizzle in the pomegranate molasses. Taste for seasoning. Transfer to a bowl and serve immediately, or transfer to an airtight container and refrigerate for up to 3 days.

Green Angel

VG, GF, NF

My diet has always been 90 percent yogurt, and I live for a great dip. This recipe scratches that itch and is totally adaptable to whatever herbs you have lying around. (At the height of spring, I might even throw ramps in.) I eat it with everything because its flavors are so adaptable: it's bright, fresh, super herbaceous, and packs such a punch. I like to add it to canned fish or chopped chicken for sandwiches, toss it as a dressing, or serve it as a dip with salty chips or lots of fresh veggies.

Add the yogurt, basil, cilantro, scallions, avocado, garlic, lemon juice, olive oil, and salt to a food processor. Process for 2 to 3 minutes, until smooth and vibrant green. Taste for seasoning. Transfer to a bowl and serve immediately, or transfer to an airtight container and refrigerate for up to 3 days.

Makes 4 cups

1 (32-ounce) container plain fat-free Greek yogurt

2 packed cups fresh basil leaves

2 packed cups fresh cilantro leaves

5 scallions, chopped

1 avocado, pitted and flesh scooped out

3 garlic cloves

¼ cup fresh lemon juice

¼ cup extra-virgin olive oil

1 tablespoon kosher salt, plus more as needed

There are a lot of herbs here, so if your food processor is on the smaller side, work in batches and stir together in a large mixing bowl.

Pesto White Bean Dip

(V, GF)

When I was working as a cook in Italy, I spent a lot of summer afternoons sitting at small cafes enjoying a glass of wine alongside bean dip and crackers. That was a formative culinary period for me, and this pesto bean dip is one of those food memories I love to re-create. It's simple in prep and execution, which means everything needs to be on point. There are lots of great store-bought pestos, which are totally welcome here, but I think this is the time to go with homemade for the ultimate experience.

Makes 3 cups

2 (15.5-ounce) cans cannellini beans, drained and rinsed

½ cup Greenery Pesto (page 73)

¼ cup fresh lemon juice

2 garlic cloves

½ tablespoon kosher salt

Add the cannellini beans, pesto, lemon juice, garlic, and salt to a food processor. Process until smooth, stopping to scrape the sides as needed, about 1 minute. Taste for seasoning and add cold water as needed to reach a hummus-like consistency. Transfer to a bowl and serve immediately, or transfer to an airtight container and refrigerate for up to 5 days.

Fava Smash

(V, GF, NF)

I grew up eating fava beans (*foul* in Arabic, pronounced like "fool"), which are a staple of the Middle Eastern diet. This dip has a lot of flavor, is very adaptable, and can easily be added to dishes as an extra source of protein. One of my favorite ways to use leftovers is warmed up and sprinkled with pepper Jack cheese for a Tex-Mex meets Lebanese take on refried beans.

Makes 4 cups

2 (15.5-ounce cans) fava beans or foul moudamas, drained and rinsed

¼ cup fresh lemon juice

3 tablespoons extra-virgin olive oil

1 garlic clove

2 teaspoons kosher salt

½ tablespoon ground cumin

Add the fava beans, lemon juice, olive oil, garlic, salt, and cumin to a food processor. Process for about 1 minute, until smooth. With the processor running, slowly stream in ¼ cup cold water. Taste for seasoning. Transfer to a bowl and serve immediately, or transfer to an airtight container and refrigerate for up to 5 days.

Toum

V, GF, NF

Since the Grocer first opened, customers have been asking to buy containers of our toum. We slather it on the shawarma, but it takes too much precision to make bulk batches for retail. With only a few ingredients, it takes care, attention, and ice-cold water to get the emulsification just right. Carefully follow this recipe for a garlicky aioli (which happens to be vegan!) that you'll be spreading on everything right away. This recipe specifically uses weight measurements because the balance is so precise. There are cup measures too if you don't have a kitchen scale, but I would encourage working by weight here.

Makes 3 cups

130 grams garlic cloves (1 cup)

1 tablespoon kosher salt

60 grams fresh lemon juice (¼ cup)

300 grams vegetable oil (1½ cups)

200 grams extra-virgin olive oil (¾ cup)

60 grams ice water (¼ cup)

1. Add the garlic and salt to a food processor. Pulse about 6 times, stopping to scrape the sides as needed, until the garlic is minced. Add 1 tablespoon of the lemon juice and process for about 30 seconds, until a rough paste forms. Add another 1 tablespoon lemon juice and process for about 45 seconds, until smooth.
2. With the processor running, slowly drizzle in ½ cup of the vegetable oil and another 1 tablespoon lemon juice. Continue alternating until both are incorporated. Drizzle in 1 tablespoon of the ice water, then ¼ cup of the olive oil, and continue the alternating pattern until both are incorporated. Transfer to an airtight container and refrigerate for up to 2 months.

Turmeric Cauliflower

V, GF, NF

Preserved lemon is a salty, tangy pickled lemon condiment used throughout the Middle East. The brine is used to retain the fresh bite of the lemons long after their growing season ends but break down the skin so the full lemon is a soft, edible, and very potent version of itself. Here it goes a long way to perk up simple roasted cauliflower for a dip that has exciting layers of flavor!

Makes 3 cups

For the cauliflower:

2 medium heads cauliflower (about 1 pound each), cut into florets

2 tablespoons extra-virgin olive oil

1 tablespoon kosher salt

1 tablespoon ground turmeric

For the dip:

½ cup tahini

¼ cup fresh lemon juice

1 preserved lemon, chopped (about ½ cup)

2 tablespoons extra-virgin olive oil

1 teaspoon kosher salt

Roughly chopped fresh parsley, for serving

1. Preheat the oven to 400°F.

2. Make the cauliflower: Add the florets to a rimmed baking sheet. Toss with the olive oil, salt, and turmeric. Transfer to the oven and bake for 30 to 40 minutes, until the cauliflower is fork-tender and lightly browned. Remove from the oven and cool completely, about 1 hour.

3. Make the dip: Add the cooled cauliflower to a food processor along with the tahini, lemon juice, preserved lemon, olive oil, and salt. Process until smooth, about 2 minutes. With the processor running, drizzle in ¼ cup cold water. Taste for seasoning. Transfer to a bowl and garnish with parsley before serving, or transfer to an airtight container and refrigerate for up to 3 days.

Orangey Date Carrot Dip

V, GF, NF

I love the natural sweetness the orange, date molasses, and carrot bring to this dip. A little tahini and garlic nudge it toward savory, the orange zest adds a perfect zing, and it's overall a well-rounded combination. We make this every year at the Grocer as a fall menu rotation, but really it would be excellent year-round served with soft pita, chips, or crudités.

1. Preheat the oven to 400°F.
2. Add the carrots to a rimmed baking sheet. Toss with the olive oil, cumin, and salt. Transfer to the oven and bake for 30 to 40 minutes, until fork-tender but not taking on too much color.
3. Add the roasted carrots to a food processor along with the orange zest and juice, tahini, date molasses, and garlic. Process for 2 minutes, or until smooth. Taste for seasoning and add cold water as needed to adjust the consistency. Transfer to a bowl and garnish with sesame seeds, pistachios, and pomegranate seeds before serving, or transfer to an airtight container and refrigerate for up to 3 days.

Makes 3 cups

2 pounds carrots, chopped into 1-inch pieces

3 tablespoons extra-virgin olive oil

1 tablespoon ground cumin

1 tablespoon kosher salt

Zest and juice (about ½ cup) of 1 large orange

½ cup tahini

¼ cup date molasses

2 garlic cloves, peeled

Sesame seeds, chopped pistachios, and pomegranate seeds, for garnish

Spicy Tomato Jam

V, GF, NF

Spicy tomato jam is the RuPaul of this book—it starts naked (tomato sauce) and the rest is drag (a little garlic, Aleppo pepper, and a few hours in hair and makeup aka the oven). We use it in everything at the Grocer—there's always a few large batches in the fridge—and you'll see this recipe pop up all over this book, in everything from Marinated Feta (page 60) to Za'atar Shakshuka (page 98) to Aleppo Garlic Shrimp Cocktail (page 173). It does take a couple hours to make the tomato sauce, so you are welcome to use store-bought marinara sauce in a pinch. But I encourage you to carve out some time to make this from scratch because the depth of flavor is unreal.

Makes 8 cups

1 cup extra-virgin olive oil

½ cup sliced garlic (from 6 cloves)

¼ cup Aleppo pepper

8 cups Edy's Tomato Sauce (page 180) or store-bought marinara sauce

1. Preheat the oven to 425°F.
2. Add the olive oil to a small saucepan over medium heat. When the oil is shimmering, add the garlic and Aleppo pepper. Reduce the heat to medium-low and simmer for about 15 minutes, until the oil is bright red and fragrant.
3. Pour the tomato sauce into a 9 by 13-inch baking dish. Stir in the oil mixture. Cover tightly with foil and poke with about 8 holes. Place on a rimmed baking sheet and transfer to the oven. Bake for about 2 hours, until thick and jammy. Cool completely, then transfer to an airtight container and refrigerate for up to 2 weeks.

You can cook this for an additional hour or two for a super thick jam (keep a careful eye on it so it doesn't burn). It can also be stored in the freezer for up to 3 months. Slowly thaw in the refrigerator before using.

Everything Salmon Salad

P, GF, NF

I am a big fish salad fan, and this salad is one of my favorites. Swapping in Greek yogurt for mayonnaise makes it feel lighter, and the cucumber, scallions, and parsley bring a freshness to a dish that can skew very rich. And I can't ever eat fish without plenty of lemon! It's such a great way to get protein, but it's still light and delicious. I often make it with salmon scraps or leftover cooked salmon, but it can also be made with canned fish (salmon or pretty much anything else!). Store-bought everything bagel seasoning will work great here, but my everything seasoning, spiked with peppery nigella seeds, takes it up a notch so it's worth the extra effort to make your own. You can slather it onto a freshly toasted bagel, but I love spreading it on seeded crackers or just dragging warm pita through it.

Makes 3 cups

1 pound salmon fillets

Kosher salt

1 cup plain fat-free Greek yogurt

¼ cup seeded and finely chopped cucumber

¼ cup chopped fresh parsley

¼ cup sliced scallions

¼ cup drained capers

2 tablespoons Edy's Everything Seasoning (page 23) or store-bought everything bagel seasoning

2 tablespoons fresh lemon juice

2 tablespoons extra-virgin olive oil

1. Preheat the oven to 400°F. Line a rimmed baking sheet with parchment paper.

2. Place the salmon on the prepared baking sheet and season with salt. Bake for 10 to 12 minutes, until cooked through. Remove from the oven and use a fork to flake the fish into small chunks. Set aside to cool for about 20 minutes.

3. While the salmon is cooling, add the yogurt, cucumber, parsley, scallions, capers, everything seasoning, lemon juice, and olive oil to a large bowl. Mix well, then fold in the cooled salmon. Transfer to a serving bowl and serve immediately, or transfer to an airtight container and refrigerate for up to 3 days.

Charred Baba Ganoush

V, GF, NF

This is a fast and easy dish. Charring the eggplant on the stove or under the broiler gives the dish its signature smoky flavor, and letting it steam gets the flesh nicely soft. After that, a simple mix of ingredients makes for a perfect dip, side dish, sandwich spread, or salad topping.

Makes 3 cups

1. Poke the eggplants all over with a fork, concentrating on the firmest areas at the top and bottom. Roast the eggplants over an open flame on the stovetop for 15 minutes, flipping every 5 minutes to ensure char on all sides of the eggplants. (For an electric oven, place under the broiler for 15 minutes, flipping every 5 minutes.) Place the charred eggplants into a bowl and cover tightly with plastic wrap. Let steam for 20 minutes. Remove the eggplants from the bowl and peel the outer skins off (some charred bits are fine), revealing the flesh.

2. In a large bowl, combine the lemon juice, tahini, olive oil, salt, cumin, garlic, and the eggplant. Use a wooden spoon to stir and mash everything together. Transfer to a bowl and serve immediately, or transfer to an airtight container and refrigerate for up to 3 days.

2 large eggplants, about 12 ounces each

½ cup fresh lemon juice

½ cup tahini

¼ cup extra-virgin olive oil

1 tablespoon kosher salt

1 tablespoon ground cumin

2 to 3 garlic cloves, grated

Spicy Fig Jam

V, GF, NF

This is one of the biggest sellers at the Grocer and an absolute staple for any catering event. It's the MVP of any cheese board or charcuterie spread, and I especially love it over grilled halloumi. Dried figs get revived with the help of lots of sesame and Aleppo pepper. It's just a quick zap in the blender for the easiest jam you'll ever make!

Makes 4 cups

4 cups dried figs (20 ounces)

½ cup white sesame seeds

1 to 2 tablespoons Aleppo pepper

1 teaspoon kosher salt

1. Add the figs to a large bowl and pour 3 cups boiling water on top to submerge them. Place a plate face down on top of the bowl to trap the steam and let sit for 1 to 2 hours, until the figs are soft.

2. Add the figs and soaking water to a blender. Blend on high speed, stopping to scrape down the sides as needed, until a thick paste forms. Add the paste to a small saucepan over medium-low heat. Stir in the sesame seeds, Aleppo pepper, and salt. Bring to a simmer and cook for about 20 minutes, stirring occasionally, until thick and jammy. Remove from the heat and cool completely. Transfer to an airtight container and refrigerate for up to 2 weeks.

If you need Spicy Fig Jam in a pinch for one of these recipes, just mix a jar of store-bought fig jam with 2 tablespoons sesame seeds and 1 tablespoon Aleppo pepper!

Grab the Lactaid
Because Who Can Live Without Labneh?

Plain Labneh & Garlicky Labneh

VG, GF, NF

Labneh is everything to me. It's the butter to my bread, the ketchup to my fries. When we came to the US, I couldn't find the sharp, tangy labneh I loved in Lebanon, so in my twenties I came up with this recipe to get as close to it as possible. Labneh is now found in some artisanal grocery stores, but making it at home is so easy. (Plus, homemade always tastes better.) Most of the activity of this recipe is leaving it alone to strain in the fridge—I'm still always shocked at how much whey comes out by the next morning. But the reward is a thick and flavorful labneh that's equally great as a spread or a dip.

Plain Labneh

Makes 8 cups

2 (32-ounce) containers plain fat-free Greek yogurt
½ cup fresh lemon juice
½ cup extra-virgin olive oil
3 tablespoons kosher salt

1. Add the yogurt, lemon juice, olive oil, and salt to a medium bowl and whisk to combine. Taste for seasoning.
2. Set a colander over a large bowl and line with cheesecloth—there should be about an inch of cloth hanging over the edge. Scrape the yogurt mixture into the cheesecloth and fold the cloth over the top to completely cover. Store in the refrigerator to **let drain overnight or up to 24 hours.** The strained labneh can be refrigerated in an airtight container for up to 2 weeks.

Garlicky Labneh

Follow the recipe for Plain Labneh, whisking 3 grated garlic cloves in with the rest of the ingredients.

Marinated Labneh Balls

(VG, GF, NF)

When I was growing up, my dad would go to Zahlé, the third-largest city in Lebanon, known for its wine and labneh balls. They were made with goat's milk—I can still taste them—and I would wait in anticipation for him to get home so I could dive in. I've always been a little disappointed by labneh balls in the US—they're usually imported instead of fresh-made—so this recipe was my solution. It's the same as making labneh, but with extra draining for a very firm base. Once you roll them up, just coat them in your favorite seasoning (I have suggestions here for three different versions, but feel free to use what you have in your pantry!). Let them marinate in oil to improve in flavor and you'll be flying through these by the jarful in no time!

Makes 20 to 25 balls

½ cup dried mint

½ cup za'atar

½ cup Aleppo pepper

Plain Labneh (page 55; see note) or 8 cups store-bought labneh

Extra-virgin olive oil

1. If you're making labneh from scratch, extend the draining time from **24 hours to 3 to 4 days** to make the base for labneh balls. For store-bought labneh, drain for **2 to 3 days**.

2. Add the mint, za'atar, and Aleppo pepper to separate small plates. Scoop 2 tablespoons of labneh together and roll into balls. (Gloves come in handy here to avoid making a mess, or you can rub oil on your hands to prevent sticking!) Roll the balls in one spice (for separate jars) or a mixture of all of them. Fill quart jars with labneh balls, mixing and matching as desired, then fill with olive oil to cover. If the labneh balls are sticky, feel free to add some olive oil to the jar while adding the balls.

Crumble labneh balls on salad or over toast for a quick and delicious lunch sure to impress. Make sure to save the flavorful oil for dressings!

Ricotta Three Ways

I really fell in love with ricotta during my time in Italy—the creamy richness felt brand-new compared to grocery brands I had tried. So when I came back, I got to work making my own at home, which quickly became an Edy's Grocer staple! (Plus, if you're like me and never nailed bread making, homemade ricotta can be your party trick.) Because Italians use ricotta interchangeably as a savory and sweet ingredient, I wanted to do a version of both here. For savory, I add lemon zest, fresh thyme, and the bite of fresh black pepper. And for sweet, I rely on rosewater and honey, two simple ingredients that bring it to life.

The Mother Ricotta
VG, GF, NF

Makes 1 pound or 2 cups

1 gallon whole milk

1 quart heavy cream

3 tablespoons kosher salt

½ cup fresh lemon juice

½ cup apple cider vinegar

1. Add the milk, cream, and salt to a large saucepan over low heat. Warm, stirring occasionally, until a thermometer reads 195°F. Remove from the heat and stir in the lemon juice and vinegar. Let the mixture sit until curds form, about 15 minutes.

2. Set a colander over a large bowl and line with cheesecloth—there should be about an inch of cloth hanging over the edge. Strain the ricotta into the cheesecloth and discard the whey (the liquid) from the bowl. Gather the sides of the cheesecloth and twist into a tight ball of curds. Set the colander back over the bowl and leave the ricotta to strain in the cheesecloth for about 2 hours, until fully cooled. Transfer to an airtight container and refrigerate for up to 2 weeks.

Rosey Ricotta
VG, GF, NF

1 pound Mother Ricotta (see above) or store-bought ricotta, at room temperature

2 tablespoons rosewater

2 tablespoons honey

1 tablespoon extra-virgin olive oil

½ tablespoon kosher salt

Add the ricotta, rosewater, honey, olive oil, and salt to a medium bowl. Use a rubber spatula to fold it all together until incorporated. Serve immediately or refrigerate in an airtight container for up to 2 weeks.

Edy's Tip: *Serve with cake, French toast, waffles, or crepes instead of whipped cream!*

Peppery Thyme Ricotta

VG, GF, NF

Add the ricotta, lemon zest, olive oil, thyme, pepper, and salt to a medium bowl. Use a rubber spatula to fold it all together until incorporated. Serve immediately or refrigerate in an airtight container for up to 2 weeks.

Edy's Tip: *Fold into or serve on top of any of your favorite pasta dishes!*

1 pound Mother Ricotta (page 58) or store-bought ricotta, at room temperature

Zest of 1 lemon

2 tablespoons extra-virgin olive oil

1 tablespoon fresh thyme leaves

½ tablespoon freshly ground black pepper

½ tablespoon kosher salt

Marinated Feta

VG, GF, NF

I came up with this on a whim, kind of out of necessity. In the days before we opened the Grocer, I accidentally ordered a huge can of feta and had to find a way to use it. This easy marinade plays well with the salty feta and keeps it fresh longer—although it's so popular in the store, our biggest issue has become how to keep up with the demand! Most of the ingredients are interchangeable, but the tomato jam is an absolute must—the sweet richness of the jam marries well with the salty freshness of the feta. Just trust me!

Makes 3 cups

½ cup Spicy Tomato Jam (page 50) or store-bought marinara sauce

¼ cup extra-virgin olive oil

¼ cup chopped pitted Kalamata olives

1 tablespoon black sesame seeds

1 tablespoon Aleppo pepper

1 tablespoon fresh thyme leaves

1 pound plain feta cheese, draine

Add the tomato jam, olive oil, olives, sesame seeds, Aleppo pepper, and thyme to a medium airtight container. Whisk to combine. Crumble in the cheese and stir to combine. Cover tightly and marinate in the refrigerator for at least 1 hour or up to 2 weeks. Serve cold or at room temperature.

Raw Shankleesh & Marinated Shankleesh

VG, GF, NF

Shankleesh is a funky Lebanese cheese, super sharp and pungent, almost like a blue cheese. It's made from labneh balls that have been fermented, and in Lebanon you eat it raw with fresh onions and tomatoes. At the Grocer, I put a twist on those flavors with a marinated shankleesh mixed with caramelized onions and spicy tomato jam. Both versions are included here. Shankleesh takes some seeking out but can reliably be found in Middle Eastern stores and fine cheese shops (the flavor is really worth the effort!). If you're coming up empty, you can substitute feta!

Raw Shankleesh

Add the tomato, scallion, and olive oil to a medium bowl. Mix well. Fold in the shankleesh. Serve immediately or transfer to an airtight container and refrigerate for up to 2 weeks.

Makes 2 cups

⅔ cup diced tomato

⅓ cup thinly sliced scallion

¼ cup extra-virgin olive oil

5 ounces shankleesh, crumbled

Marinated Shankleesh

1. Heat ¼ cup of the olive oil in a large nonstick skillet over medium heat. When the oil is shimmering, add the onions. Sauté, stirring often, for 20 to 25 minutes, until golden brown and jammy. Transfer to a medium bowl and cool for 25 minutes.
2. Add the crumbled shankleesh to a medium bowl. Fold in the cooled onions, tomato jam, and the remaining 1 tablespoon olive oil. Serve immediately or transfer to an airtight container and refrigerate for up to 2 weeks.

Makes 2 cups

¼ cup plus 1 tablespoon extra-virgin olive oil

4 cups thinly sliced onion (from about 6 medium yellow onions)

5 ounces shankleesh, crumbled

⅓ cup Spicy Tomato Jam (page 50) or store-bought marinara sauce

Baked Mediterranean Feta

VG, GF, NF

Feta, one of Lebanon's favorite cheeses, is so versatile. This baked feta is a favorite of mine around the holidays because it's so warm and inviting, communal to dip into, and always a staple of the Brown Paper Board. There are a lot of salty and briny flavors here, but they all mellow and meld during the baking process, which transforms this into a perfectly creamy and savory dish ready for spreading on crackers and bread.

1. Preheat the oven to 350°F.
2. Arrange the cheese in an 8 by 8-inch baking pan. Top with the tomatoes, olives, capers, and rosemary. (Keep the tomatoes whole—they'll soften and burst in the oven.) Drizzle over the olive oil and season with the pepper and nigella seeds. Bake for 15 to 18 minutes, until the cheese is golden brown and bubbly. Serve immediately with toasted pita or baguette slices.

Serves 8

2 pounds plain feta cheese, preferably Bulgarian, cubed

30 cherry tomatoes

½ cup pitted Kalamata olives, quartered

¼ cup drained capers

2 rosemary sprigs

¼ cup extra-virgin olive oil

½ teaspoon freshly ground black pepper

1 teaspoon nigella seeds

Toasted pita or baguette slices, for serving

To feed a crowd, double this recipe and bake in a 9 by 13-inch baking pan.

Edy's Tip

Za'atar Goat Cheese

(VG, GF, NF)

A version of this started during my catering days when I would set out a log of goat cheese and spread za'atar paste on top. At the end of one party, I packed up the leftover cheese into a container and the next day I mashed it up to eat it. I realized it was far better as a spread with za'atar swirled throughout and never set out a log again. This is a great thing to make ahead and refrigerate, letting the flavors meld. Just be sure to let it sit at room temperature for 30 minutes before serving for maximum spreadability.

Makes 2 cups

1 (10.5-ounce) log goat cheese, at room temperature

2 tablespoons extra-virgin olive oil

1 teaspoon kosher salt

⅓ cup Za'atar Paste (page 73) or store-bought za'atar paste

Add the goat cheese, olive oil, and salt to a medium bowl. Use a spatula (or handheld mixer) to fold everything together. Add the za'atar paste in increments, folding to fully incorporate. Transfer to an airtight container and refrigerate for up to 2 weeks. To serve, scoop into a bowl or large ramekin and serve with a cheese knife for spreading.

"In a Pickle"
Marinating and Pickling

Sizzling Sun-Dried Tomatoes

V, GF, NF

While I was working in Italy, I saw people sun-drying their own tomatoes all over Tuscany. The tomatoes in Italy are like nothing else, and biting into a sun-dried tomato was like getting punched in the face by flavor. In this easy four-ingredient recipe, the tomatoes are infused with an herby, spicy harissa seasoning and plenty of rich olive oil for a dish that is more than the sum of its parts.

Add the olive oil to a small saucepan over high heat and heat to 350°F. While the oil heats, add the cumin seeds and harissa seasoning to a medium heat-safe bowl. Pour the hot oil over the spices and let them sizzle and mingle for about 5 minutes, until very fragrant. Add the tomatoes to the bowl. Cool completely, about 30 minutes, then transfer to a sterilized pint jar, topping off with more oil as needed, and refrigerate for at least 24 hours and up to 4 months.

Makes 2 cups

1 cup extra-virgin olive oil, plus more as needed

½ tablespoon cumin seeds

1 tablespoon Herby Harissa Seasoning (page 23)

8 ounces sun-dried tomatoes

Beiruti Balila

V, GF, NF

To me, nothing is more delicious than a perfectly marinated chickpea. I like to make huge batches of this recipe and garnish almost every dish with it. It adds a new dimension sprinkled on top of fatteh or salads, mixed in with cooked grains, as a topping for proteins, or even as the main protein itself. Balila is huge in Beirut and is almost always on the table. I like to use canned chickpeas here, which are firmer and extend the longevity of the dish.

Makes 3 cups

2 (15.5-ounce) cans chickpeas, drained and rinsed

½ cup fresh lemon juice (from 3 to 4 lemons)

¼ cup extra-virgin olive oil

2 to 3 garlic cloves, grated

2 tablespoons dried parsley

1 tablespoon ground cumin

1 tablespoon smoked paprika

1 teaspoon kosher salt

Add the chickpeas, lemon juice, olive oil, garlic, parsley, cumin, paprika, and salt to a large bowl. Mix well and taste for seasoning. Transfer to a bowl and serve immediately or marinate in the refrigerator for up to 1 week. To serve, heat gently in a saucepan over low heat or serve cold.

Marinated Olives

When I was growing up in the Koura area of North Lebanon, olive land was the most prized possession. My grandfather Afif looked forward to the olive harvest and spent all year tending to his trees. Teita Odette would pray for rain so we would get extra olives. The deep care and attention was so beautiful to see. After the harvest, he would keep some olives to marinate, make olive oil from the rest, and make soap with the discards. Distributing the rewards to his family was his way of showing his love. In 2018, I got to go back to Lebanon and do one last olive harvest with him as an adult. These marinated olives always remind me of our time together.

Marinated Green Olives

Makes 3 cups

2 cups green olives (with pits), any type, drained and rinsed

1 cup extra-virgin olive oil

3 garlic cloves, peeled

1 lemon, peeled in long strips and halved

1 teaspoon dried mint

Add the olives, olive oil, garlic, and lemon peel to a small saucepan, along with half of the peeled lemon and the juice from the other half of the lemon. Set over medium heat, bring to a simmer, and cook for 8 to 12 minutes, until deeply fragrant. Remove from the heat. Discard the lemon half but keep the peel. Let the mixture cool for 15 minutes, then stir in the mint. Serve warm or cool completely, then refrigerate in an airtight container for up to 3 months.

Marinated Kalamata Olives

Makes 3 cups

2 cups pitted Kalamata olives, drained and rinsed

1 cup extra-virgin olive oil

4 sprigs thyme

2 sprigs rosemary

1 teaspoon freshly ground black pepper

1 orange, peeled in long strips and halved

Add the olives, olive oil, thyme, rosemary, pepper, and orange peel to a small saucepan. Squeeze the juice from one half of the orange into the saucepan. (Reserve the other half for another use.) Set over medium heat, bring to a simmer, and cook for 8 to 12 minutes, until deeply fragrant. Remove from the heat. Discard the orange half but leave the peel and sprigs. Serve warm or cool completely, then refrigerate in an airtight container for up to 3 months.

Pickle It Your Way

Both of my grandmothers were pickling machines, stocking up on summer produce to last through the winter. I didn't get into pickling until much later, in my twenties, when I was working as a private chef for a family in the Hamptons. With the abundance of gorgeous summer produce, my ancestral training kicked in and I started pickling everything in sight. These are a few of my favorites, including a very Southern US–influenced pickled shrimp that I learned while working a pop-up dinner years ago. The base brine recipe will work perfectly for whatever you have on hand and want to preserve!

Each makes 2 quarts

The Mother Brine

V, GF, NF

Makes 4 cups brine, enough for 2 quarts pickles

1 cup white distilled vinegar
2 cups apple cider vinegar
½ cup kosher salt
½ cup sugar

8 bay leaves
2 tablespoons pickling spice mix
1 tablespoon black peppercorns

Add the white vinegar, apple cider vinegar, salt, sugar, bay leaves, pickling spice, peppercorns, and 1 cup water to a medium saucepan over medium heat. Stir to combine, bring to a simmer, and cook for 8 to 10 minutes, until very fragrant.

I like this mix of vinegars, but use whatever you have on hand! I find that apple cider vinegar tends to boost the color and flavor.

Pickled Cucumbers

V, GF, NF

2 pounds whole Persian cucumbers
The Mother Brine (page 70)
5 garlic cloves

4 thyme sprigs
1 lemon, peeled in long strips and halved

Add the cucumbers to a medium bowl or 2 quart jars. Add the garlic, thyme, and lemon peel to the boiling mother brine. Squeeze the juice from one half of the lemon into the saucepan. (Reserve the other half for another use.) Pour the boiling brine over the cucumbers. Cool completely, then cover and refrigerate **for at least 3 days** or up to 1 month before serving.

Pickled Turnips

V, GF, NF

The Mother Brine (page 70)

2 pounds turnips, peeled and cut into
   thick 2-inch strips
1 raw beet, quartered

Strain the mother brine and return to a boil. Add the turnips and beet and simmer for about 8 minutes, until the turnips are fork tender. Pour into 2 quart jars. Cool completely, discard the beet quarters, then cover and refrigerate **for at least 3 days** or up to 1 month before serving.

Pickled Beets

V, GF, NF

2 pounds cooked beets, cut into wedges
The Mother Brine (page 70)

5 garlic cloves
¼ cup honey

Add the beets to a medium bowl or 2 quart jars. Add the garlic and honey to the boiling mother brine. Strain the boiling brine over the beets. Enjoy right away or cool completely, then cover and refrigerate for up to 1 month.

I always buy precooked beets to save time. I think of it as the same sort of modern convenience as canned beans.

Edy's Tip

Pickled Jardiniere

V, GF, NF

½ tablespoon nigella seeds
½ tablespoon cumin seeds
1 pound cauliflower, cut into florets
8 mini sweet peppers

12 ounces carrots, peeled and sliced into
   ½-inch-thick coins
1 celery stalk, sliced ½ inch thick
The Mother Brine (page 70)

Toast the nigella seeds and cumin seeds in a small skillet over medium heat, tossing occasionally, about 3 minutes. Add the toasted seeds, cauliflower, peppers, carrots, and celery to a medium bowl or 2 quart jars. Strain the boiling brine over the vegetable mixture. Enjoy right away or cool completely, then cover and refrigerate for up to 1 month.

The jardiniere can be made with whatever veggies you need to rescue from the fridge or any leftover crudités.

Pickled Shrimp

GF, NF

¼ cup kosher salt
1½ pounds peeled and deveined shrimp
   (tail-on)
½ batch (2 cups) Mother Brine (page 70)

½ cup extra-virgin olive oil
½ cup fresh lemon juice
4 to 5 garlic cloves

1. Prepare an ice bath. Add 4 quarts water to a large pot and bring to a boil over high heat. Stir in the salt, then add the shrimp. Poach for 3 minutes, or until bright pink and opaque. Remove the shrimp to the ice bath and set aside to cool.

2. Strain and cool the mother brine. Whisk in the olive oil, lemon juice, and garlic cloves. Add the shrimp to a medium bowl or 2 quart jars. Pour the brine over the shrimp. Enjoy right away or cool completely, then cover and refrigerate for up to 5 days.

The Fixings
Topping energy: nutty, crispy & saucy

Za'atar Paste

V, GF, NF

Za'atar paste is a must-have in Lebanon, and you'll see it pop up all over this book. It's the seasoning base of choice for marinades, rubs, dips, and dressings, and of course the foundation of manoushe, Lebanon's most popular street food and breakfast. (Thyme, the main herb in za'atar, is said to make you smarter, so moms love to feed their kids a za'atar tartine on pita on the day of a big test.) I always keep a big jar of it within arm's reach.

Stir together the za'atar and ½ cup of the olive oil in a medium bowl. Continue adding oil a few tablespoons at a time (you'll probably use all the oil) to reach a consistency similar to a runny pesto. Store in an airtight container at room temperature for up to 6 months. Stir well before using.

Makes 2 cups

1 cup Za'atar (page 23), or store-bought
1 cup extra-virgin olive oil

Greenery Pesto

V, GF

During my time cooking in Italy, pesto became a weekly practice. We'd always have lots of leftover herbs in the kitchen, and making pesto was the easiest way to make them stretch to the very end of their natural life. I still love to make pesto from scratch, using scraps and leftovers, and freeze it for a rainy day. This one is super green and punchy, but feel free to swap in whatever herbs and greens you have on hand.

Add the walnuts, arugula, basil, mint, lemon juice, garlic, salt, and pepper to a food processor. Process for about 2 minutes, stopping to scrape the sides as needed, until finely chopped. With the processor running, slowly drizzle in the olive oil. Taste for seasoning. Serve immediately or refrigerate in an airtight container for up to 1 week.

Makes 2½ cups

2 cups walnuts
2 cups arugula
2 cups fresh basil leaves
1 cup fresh mint leaves
¼ cup fresh lemon juice
4 garlic cloves
1 tablespoon kosher salt, plus more as needed
½ tablespoon freshly ground black pepper
1 cup extra-virgin olive oil

Hashweh

GF

Hashweh is a mixture of ground beef, onion, and Baharat usually cooked in a lot of fat to preserve it like a condiment. It's used in a lot of Middle Eastern cooking, as a stuffing for vegetables, in Riz a Djej (page187), on top of hummus, and inside kibbeh (page 191). It's one of the most important building blocks for Lebanese home cooks.

Makes about 4 cups

2 tablespoons extra-virgin olive oil

1 medium yellow onion, diced (about 1 cup)

1 pound ground beef (preferably 90% lean)

1 tablespoon kosher salt

1 tablespoon Baharat (page 21) or ground cumin

2 tablespoons pine nuts

Heat the olive oil in a medium skillet over medium heat. When the oil is shimmering, add the onion and cook, stirring occasionally, until translucent, about 5 minutes. Add the beef and cook, breaking it up, until cooked through, 6 to 8 minutes. Stir in the salt, baharat, and pine nuts and taste for seasoning. Cover and refrigerate until ready to use, up to 5 days.

Sesame Aleppo Breadcrumbs

V, NF

When Maria, the previous owner of what would become Edy's Grocer, was clearing out of the space before I opened the Grocer, she left me with tons of breadcrumbs. I love a challenge, so I decided to add a little zest to the backstock with lots of sesame and Aleppo pepper. Turns out I accidentally discovered my favorite breadcrumbs ever! This is a perfect topping for baked pasta dishes or finishing roasted vegetables.

Makes 2 cups

1½ cups panko breadcrumbs

½ cup white sesame seeds

¼ cup extra-virgin olive oil

2 tablespoons Aleppo pepper

1 teaspoon kosher salt

Add the breadcrumbs and sesame seeds to a medium skillet. Set over medium heat and toast, stirring constantly, until golden brown, about 5 minutes. Transfer to a medium bowl and wipe out the skillet. Add the olive oil and Aleppo pepper to the skillet and return to medium heat. Bring to a simmer and cook for about 4 minutes, until the Aleppo pepper is dark and crispy. Pour the oil mixture over the breadcrumbs, add the salt, and mix thoroughly. Cool completely in the bowl, about 30 minutes. Store in an airtight container at room temperature for up to 3 weeks.

Harissa Sour Cream

VG, GF, NF

In addition to breadcrumbs (page 74), Maria also left me with a ton of sour cream, so I mixed in my own familiar flavor: spicy harissa. When I first opened the Grocer, the menu had a few Polish items like pierogi and potato pancakes, and I leaned on this sour cream to nudge that food closer to my palate.

Add the sour cream, olive oil, harissa paste, tomato paste, and salt to a blender. Blend on low speed until smooth and bright red, about 1 minute. Taste for seasoning. Cover and refrigerate until ready to use, up to 5 days.

Makes 3 cups

3 cups sour cream

2 tablespoons extra-virgin olive oil

2 tablespoons harissa paste

2 tablespoons tomato paste

1 tablespoon kosher salt

Middle Eastern Pico de Gallo

V, GF, NF

I love Mexican food, especially the fresh salsa known as pico de gallo. This Middle Eastern version works with the same idea of freshly chopped veggies but swaps out the lime juice for briny olives. The result is much less juicy and great as a fresh topping.

Add the cucumber, tomato, and olives to a medium bowl. Toss to combine. Cover and refrigerate until ready to use, up to 3 days.

Makes 2¼ cups

1 cup finely chopped Persian cucumber (2 Persian cucumbers)

1 cup finely chopped tomato (1 medium vine tomato)

¼ cup sliced Kalamata olives

Tahini Sauce Chart

This wouldn't be a Middle Eastern cookbook without an ode to tahini. When I first moved here, I couldn't find tahini anywhere, and now it feels like it's everywhere! I've made so many variations of these sauces throughout my career, and because tahini is such a neutral taste, it can really take on any flavor. I hope all these ideas become part of your cooking vocabulary and inspire you to create more of your own!

The Mother Tahini

V, GF, NF

Each makes 2 cups

1 cup tahini
½ cup fresh lemon juice
2 garlic cloves
1 tablespoon kosher salt

Add the ingredients plus 1 cup water to a blender. Blend on low speed for about 2 minutes, stopping to scrape the sides as needed, until fully combined. Taste for seasoning and refrigerate in an airtight container for up to 1 week.

Cilantro Lime Tahini	Basil Lemon Tahini	Spicy Tahini	Sweet Tahini	Caesar Tahini Dressing
V, GF, NF	V, GF, NF	V, GF, NF	V, GF, NF	P, GF, NF
Blend with: 1 packed cup fresh cilantro with stems ¼ cup fresh lime juice	Blend with: 1 packed cup fresh basil leaves An extra ¼ cup fresh lemon juice	Blend with: 2 tablespoons harissa paste 1 tablespoon Aleppo pepper	Blend with: ⅓ cup honey	Blend with: ½ cup plain fat-free Greek yogurt ¼ cup drained capers 2 tablespoons extra-virgin olive oil 1 tablespoon Worcestershire sauce 1 teaspoon freshly ground black pepper

Vinaigrette Chart

My mom always has a simple lemon vinaigrette on hand. When I was growing up, it was our only dressing, used on everything with no variation. When I moved to America and saw a wall of dressings for the first time, it was so confusing. I had never tried any of them and they were all so different. My favorite is still the basic lemon vinaigrette, but now I use it as a perfect base to start mixing in multiple flavors. These are some of my most-used vinaigrettes.

The Mother Lemon

V, GF, NF

Each makes 2 cups

¾ cup extra-virgin olive oil
¾ cup fresh lemon juice
2 teaspoons kosher salt
2 ice cubes

Add the ingredients to a blender. Blend on high speed for about 1 minute, until fully combined. Taste for seasoning and refrigerate in an airtight container for up to 1 week.

Minty	Tangy Sumac	Sweet Pomegranate	Spicy Harissa	Garlicky	Punchy Dijon
V, GF, NF	V, GF, NF	V, GF, NF	V, GF, NF	V, GF, NF	V, GF, NF
Blend with: 1 packed cup fresh mint leaves	Blend with: ¼ cup sumac	Blend with: 3 tablespoons pomegranate molasses	Blend with: 3 tablespoons harissa paste	Blend with: 3 tablespoons Toum (page 45) or 2 garlic cloves	Blend with: 3 tablespoons Dijon mustard

Edy's Tip: *Ice cubes help with the emulsification of the dressing so it doesn't break!*

Aleppo Chili Crisp

V, GF

This is an ode to James Park, my close friend and a talented chef. He has always been my biggest cheerleader and pushed me to be who I am. Through cooking, shopping, and swapping pantry items, I taught him about Lebanese food and he taught me about Korean food. This chili crisp meets in the middle of our cultures and is one of my most-used condiments. I literally put it on everything!

Makes 3 cups

2 cups vegetable oil

18 to 20 garlic cloves, grated (about ½ cup)

5 scallions, sliced

½ cup white sesame seeds

¼ cup pine nuts or pepitas

½ cup Aleppo pepper, or more to taste

1 tablespoon nigella seeds

1 tablespoon cumin seeds

¼ cup harissa paste

1 tablespoon kosher salt

1. Heat the vegetable oil in a small saucepan over medium heat until it reaches 350°F, or until the surface ripples but isn't quite smoking yet. Using a slotted spoon or spider, lower in the garlic and scallions from a safe distance away from any oil splatter and fry, stirring occasionally, for about 6 minutes, until the garlic is browned and crispy.

2. While the oil is infusing, add the sesame seeds, pine nuts, Aleppo pepper, nigella seeds, and cumin seeds to a medium skillet over medium heat. Toast, stirring often, for about 6 minutes, until very fragrant and the pine nuts are golden. Transfer to a medium bowl to cool slightly.

3. When the infused oil is ready, pour it over the seed mixture and let it sizzle away. Stir in the harissa paste and salt until dissolved. Let the chili crisp cool for about 30 minutes before serving or cool completely and refrigerate in an airtight container for up to 1 month.

Fried Nut Mix

V, GF

Making this always reminds me of sitting in the kitchen, watching Teita Odette standing at the stove frying nuts, a recurring scene in my childhood. Nuts are expensive and delicate, so you have to stand guard and watch your temperature and oil carefully. But the result is the ultimate crispy topping to so many dishes; you'll see it all throughout the book, like the perfect finishing touch to Riz a Djej (page 187) or a variety of Fatteh (page 197). This is my favorite mix, but feel free to swap in whatever nuts you prefer or have lying around.

Add the vegetable oil to a large skillet over medium-low heat. When the oil is shimmering, add the almonds and fry for about 3 minutes, stirring often to make sure they don't burn, until lightly toasted. Add the cashews and continue frying and stirring for about 3 minutes, until lightly toasted. Add the pistachios and continue frying and stirring for about 2 minutes. Add the pepitas and keep going for about 3 minutes. Finally, add the pine nuts and salt and continue frying and stirring for about 3 minutes, until everything is golden brown. Remove from the heat and stir in the sesame seeds. Transfer to a plate to cool. Store in an airtight container at room temperature for up to 1 month.

Makes 2¼ cups

2 tablespoons vegetable oil

½ cup almonds

½ cup cashews

½ cup shelled pistachios

½ cup pepitas

2 tablespoons pine nuts

2 teaspoons kosher salt

2 tablespoons white sesame seeds

Sabaho

**The Breakfast
Fuel You
Need to Start
Your Day**

Sabaho, Bonjour, Good morning,
Buongiorno a tutti

My love for coffee started at a young age because I saw how it always brought people together. There's a saying in Lebanon, whenever you pass by a neighbor, a friend, or even a stranger, they will shout "hawel shrab qahwah?" which means come by and have some coffee. It's how the community gathers. Old men sit on stools outside shops playing backgammon and drinking coffee, and women cluster on benches and patios to smoke cigarettes, sip coffee, play cards, and dish out gossip. Coffee has always been an excuse to connect.

Growing up, I would scurry home from church to sit with my Teita Odette on her balcony while she sipped on her freshly brewed Turkish coffee. Her ritual of making Turkish coffee was so special. All it took was a little hand pot, some water, low heat, and a metal spoon just long enough to not burn your fingertips. But Odette would stand over her gas stove, stirring the coffee slowly until it just became foamy on the top, not leaving it for a second longer and risking any boilover. She would grab her oval silver tray with the carved-out handles and arrange a stack of the little Turkish coffee cups and saucers on it, along with McVitie's Digestive biscuits, some spoons, and a little jar of sugar. With her hair freshly blown out, she would walk outside, ready to sip, smoke, and chitchat with her sisters and girlfriends.

For the younger generation coffee didn't just mean Turkish coffee. It also meant Lebanese white coffee, the nickname for a digestive drink made of hot water spiked with orange blossom. Technically it's closer to a tea, but Lebanese people call it white coffee because it's served just like coffee, in little decorative cups, beautifully hand painted with red, blue, or green. On hot summer nights in Anfeh, when my parents were hosting a dinner party, my favorite part was sitting outside on the balcony acting like I was playing with my yellow Game Boy, but actually eavesdropping on the gossip from the few lingering guests. They would sip on white coffee, laugh, reminisce about old times, and worry about the future of their country.

When we immigrated to the US, I felt like my parents had lost that sense of community. They didn't have anyone to invite over for coffee and gossip. Instead, we would drive through Dunkin' Donuts on Saturday mornings. My parents would take a sip and yell, "This American coffee is so watered down, how do they drink this stuff?!"

Sometimes I forgot—as hard as this new life was for my sister and me—that moving was even harder on my parents. They were in their late thirties, they had left everything and everyone they loved behind, and they were trying to navigate a whole new world without speaking any English. Slowly, they started to make friends and would meet at the local Starbucks, a far cry from the communal gathering in Lebanon, but good enough to connect for an hour or two.

This longing for coffee and community never made sense to me until I became an adult. I finally had my first sip of coffee in Orvieto, Italy, at age eighteen. I was interning at a restaurant and the sous-chef made me do it. ("If you want to be one of us, you have to drink espresso with us.") So, every day I would show up to work and the whole staff would sit around the bar, drink espresso, and chat about the prep we had for the day, what we ate last night, and what city we were visiting next. This is when I started to understand that coffee was more than just a drink; it was also an opportunity to pause.

I left the espresso habit back in Italy, but cold brew quickly became my drug of choice in Brooklyn. When opening Edy's Grocer, I knew our coffee program had to be special to compete in the New York market. I dreamed of a coffee window where customers could walk up (kind of like my family's Dunkin' Donuts days) and order a coffee and pastry without having to wait in line. It brings me so much joy to be able to lean out the window, serve, and watch my community sit outside under the lemon sign enjoying their coffee and gossip. It's those moments when Brooklyn starts to feel a little like Anfeh. Following are my takes on a perfect batch of cold brew, a strong pot of Turkish coffee, and a simple version of white coffee that can be served hot or cold. These help me to find community and a sense of belonging and worth wherever I am, and I hope they'll do the same for you. So what do you say, shall we grab some coffee?

Edy's Cold Brew

V, GF, NF

Makes 10 cups

8 ounces coarsely
  ground coffee
10 cups cold filtered
  water
Ice, for serving
Milk, cream, and/or
  simple syrup (page
  230), for serving
Special equipment:
  cheesecloth and
  kitchen twine

1. Lay a double layer of cheesecloth over a small bowl. Scoop the ground coffee into the center of the cheesecloth. Gather the corners of the cloth around the coffee, making a large sachet, and tie tightly with twine. Place the sachet into a large pitcher or container and pour over the cold water. Cover the container and let it brew in the refrigerator **for 12 to 36 hours**. The longer it brews, the stronger the coffee will be. Remove the sachet from the pitcher and strain the concentrate through a sieve into your desired serving container.
2. Fill a glass with ice, then add equal parts cold brew concentrate and water. Taste and adjust as needed. Add milk, cream, or simple syrup to taste.
3. Cover the concentrate and store in the refrigerator for up to 2 weeks.

Edy's White Coffee

V, GF, NF

Serves 4

4 cups cold water
½ cup orange blossom
  water
½ cup agave nectar or
  honey

1. To serve hot, add the water, orange blossom water, and agave to a small saucepan over medium heat. Simmer, stirring occasionally, for about 5 minutes, until everything dissolves. Serve immediately in small coffee cups.
2. To serve cold, add the water, orange blossom water, and agave to a small pitcher. Stir until everything dissolves. Serve in glasses filled with ice.

Edy's Turkish Coffee

V, GF, NF

1. Bring the water to a boil in a small saucepan or Turkish coffee pot. Remove from the heat. Add the Turkish coffee, 1 tablespoon at a time so it doesn't boil over, then return to medium heat and simmer for 2 to 3 minutes, until foamy on top.
2. Divide the coffee among espresso cups and serve with sugar cubes.

Serves 4 to 6

2 cups water
½ cup Turkish coffee
Sugar cubes, for serving

To Natacha

Living above a bakery was one of the highlights of my childhood. Natacha—my older sister—and I would be excited to wake up for school. We slipped on our school uniforms, grabbed our backpacks, and made our way downstairs to Samar's Bakery.

Winter mornings were brutal in Anfeh, and we lived on the main road about two thousand feet away from the Mediterranean Sea with its harsh seasonal winds. Samar was the owner and head baker, and she started her day at 5 a.m., measuring, mixing, and kneading the manoushe dough. By the time we walked through the door, she had the oven blazing. She would portion the dough into balls and drop them on an old scale balanced with a metal weight. The scale would rock up and down while she made sure each portion was the same size. Then she dusted the sheeter machine, made for flattening the dough, with a perfect burst of flour, evenly spread over the belt so nothing would stick. Watching her use flour was like watching an artist at work. She started flattening the dough with her fingers, then fed it through the sheeter a few times until it was the perfect thickness. All day she would roll batches of dough, waiting for the next customer to come and order their manoushe.

As we were waiting for the school bus, Samar would let my sister and me make mini manoushes, spread some za'atar paste on them, and bake them in the hot oven. I was short, so she would pick me up and narrate what was happening in the oven. When the dough started bubbling, she grabbed her well-worn pizza peel, slid it into the oven, gave it a quick twist, and popped out the mini manoushe. The smell of the za'atar paste was intoxicating, and the sound of the bread crackling with oil and sesame seeds was music to my ears. "Quickly," she would say, "eat it before the bus arrives." I wouldn't even stop to take a breath as I inhaled that hot, oily dough with its mix of flavors and textures. I mean, how could you not look forward to getting up for school after a morning like that?

After we moved to America, Natacha and I grew closer. She was the only one who understood me and what we were struggling through: learning English, fitting in, and adjusting to a new lifestyle. She was my rock, and she guided me through our new life. She spoke the best English in our household, so she became our de facto translator for everything from parent-teacher conferences to calling the utility companies. (It was a surprise to no one when she later became a lawyer, and she is still my guide through all my major life choices, personal and professional.)

Year after year, when I touch down in Beirut, my first stop is always Samar's Bakery, which is still right where I left it. It always brings me so much joy to taste the manoushe, one of my earliest culinary memories, for what feels like the first time again. I carry on the tradition, selling manoushe out of the side window of Edy's Grocer to the early-morning customers starting their day in Greenpoint. I love to play with creative flavors and toppings, but we always have the classic za'atar on the menu. And, of course, I pause to have one myself, piping hot and slick with oil. It's one of the many ways I keep my connection to my home, my traditions, and, most of all, my sister.

Manoushe Three Ways

Serves 4

Za'atar Manoushe
VG, NF

1. Preheat the oven to 450°F. Line a rimmed baking sheet with parchment paper.
2. Arrange the naan on the prepared baking sheet. Spread 3 tablespoons of the za'atar paste on each one. Bake for about 6 minutes, until the edges are golden and the naan has absorbed the za'atar paste. Divide among plates and top with the Middle Eastern Pico de Gallo. Serve immediately.

4 pieces naan

¾ cup Za'atar Paste (page 73) or store-bought za'atar paste

1 cup Middle Eastern Pico de Gallo (page 75) or store-bought pico de gallo

Spicy Cheese Manoushe
VG, NF

1. Preheat the oven to 450°F. Line a rimmed baking sheet with parchment paper.
2. Arrange the naan on the prepared baking sheet. Add the Akkawi, mozzarella, feta, and Aleppo pepper to a medium bowl. Mix to combine. Divide the cheese evenly over the top of the naan. Bake for about 6 minutes, until the cheese is melted and bubbling. Divide the naan among plates and drizzle with honey. Serve immediately.

4 pieces naan

8 ounces Akkawi cheese (see note) or ricotta salata, shredded

8 ounces mozzarella cheese, shredded

4 ounces feta cheese, crumbled

3 tablespoons Aleppo pepper

Honey, for serving

Edy's Tip: *Akkawi is a Lebanese soft cheese with a salty flavor and slightly chewy texture. It can be found in Middle Eastern grocers or substituted with ricotta salata.*

(cont.)

Spicy Fig Jam & Ricotta Manoushe
VG, NF

4 pieces naan

½ cup Spicy Fig Jam (page 54) or store-bought fig jam

½ cup The Mother Ricotta (page 58) or store-bought ricotta

Freshly ground black pepper, for serving

1. Preheat the oven to 450°F. Line a rimmed baking sheet with parchment paper.

2. Arrange the naan on the prepared baking sheet. Spread 2 tablespoons of the fig jam over each piece of naan. Dollop 2 tablespoons of the ricotta on each piece. Bake for about 6 minutes, until the ricotta is melted. Divide the naan among plates and finish with plenty of black pepper. Serve immediately.

Edy's Tip: The fig and ricotta manoushe should be served immediately, but the other two can be made ahead. Bake, cool completely without the toppings, wrap tightly with plastic wrap, and freeze for up to 1 month. Reheat in the oven until warm, then finish with the toppings.

Pop up at the Grocer with James Park

Labneh Toasts

I love labneh toast. I grew up eating it a lot (we called it *tartine* in French), and when we moved to the US, my mom would often pack it in my lunch. My dad, Simon, loved a labneh toast as a quick meal, and his favorite version is here. The spicy version is inspired by my friend James Park, who got me addicted to chili crisp. And the Grocer's brand manager, Bella Xia, who loves all things sweet, came up with the sweet version.

Serves 4

Simon's Toast
VG, NF

¼ cup Plain or Garlicky Labneh (page 55)
4 toasted mini pitas, for serving
3 tablespoons Middle Eastern Pico de Gallo (page 75) or store-bought pico de gallo

2 teaspoons Za'atar Paste (page 73) or store-bought za'atar paste

Spicy Toast
VG, NF

¼ cup Plain or Garlicky Labneh (page 55)
4 toasted mini pitas, for serving

2 tablespoons Aleppo Chili Crisp (page 78)

Sweet Toast
VG

¼ cup Plain Labneh (page 55)
4 toasted mini pitas, for serving
1 tablespoon chopped pistachios

2 teaspoons chopped fresh mint
Honey, for drizzling

Spread the labneh on each pita, then sprinkle or drizzle the toppings before serving.

Fast Croissants Chart

These have been my go-to ever since I was a kid. When I moved to America, I thought Pillsbury dough was a miracle. I had never seen something like that in Lebanon, and it opened so many doors to play and experiment in the kitchen. These four versions are my favorites, but they really can be made with whatever you want. (They also freeze well after baking—just thaw them in the oven for a few minutes for a perfect all-day snack.) I'm partial to the Pillsbury all-vegetable shortening pie crust, but use whatever brand you love the most.

Makes 16 bites

1 store-bought pie crust, thawed if frozen

Filling of choice (see chart below)

1 large egg

1 tablespoon heavy cream

Garnish of choice (see chart below)

1. Preheat the oven to 350°F. Line a rimmed baking sheet with parchment paper.
2. Use a rolling pin to stretch the crust into a 10-inch circle. Spread the filling over the crust, leaving a ½-inch border. Slice the crust into quarters, then each quarter into fourths to create 16 even wedges. Roll into mini croissants, starting from the wide edge to the tip. Place each croissant on the prepared baking sheet.
3. Whisk the egg and cream together in a small bowl. Brush the top of each croissant with the egg mixture, then top with any garnishes. Bake for 10 to 15 minutes, until puffed and golden brown. Serve warm.

	Za'atar	Za'atar & Goat Cheese	Mortadella & Cheese	Nutella
	VG, NF	VG, NF	NF	VG
Filling	½ cup Za'atar Paste (page 73) or store-bought za'atar paste	½ cup Za'atar Goat Cheese (page 64)	4 slices mortadella and 5 thin slices cheddar cheese	½ cup Nutella and 2 tablespoons chopped pistachios
Garnish	Aleppo pepper	nigella seeds	Edy's Everything Seasoning (page 23)	sesame seeds

Foul & Balila

V, GF, NF

I grew up just outside the city of Tripoli, where there were lots of street vendors. One of the most popular items in the morning was foul and balila, fava beans and chickpeas. It was a perfect breakfast for the city's workforce, cheap and filling, fast and easy. During Greek Orthodox Lent, we had to avoid meat and dairy, so Teita Odette would make this for us as an easy breakfast. It's great warm or cold and it's especially amazing with a runny egg on top.

Serves 4 to 6

3 tablespoons extra-
   virgin olive oil
2 garlic cloves, grated
4 scallions, thinly sliced
2 (15.5-ounce) cans
   fava beans or foul
   moudamas, drained
   and rinsed
2 (15.5-ounce) cans
   chickpeas, drained and
   rinsed
2 tablespoons ground
   cumin
1 tablespoon kosher salt
¾ cup fresh lemon juice
Chopped fresh parsley,
   for serving

Add the olive oil to a medium saucepan over medium heat. When the oil is shimmering, add the garlic and scallions. Sauté for about 4 minutes, until the scallions are soft and fragrant. Add the fava beans, chickpeas, cumin, and salt. Stir and simmer for about 5 minutes, until warmed through. Add the lemon juice and ½ cup water. Simmer for 10 to 12 minutes, until the beans are swollen and most of the liquid cooks off. Serve warm or cold with a sprinkle of parsley.

Rosewater Raspberry Dutch Baby

VG, NF

When I worked in the kitchen at Danny Meyer's North End Grill in lower Manhattan, we had a lemon Dutch baby on the menu. It was the most popular brunch item, fragrant and beautiful. This version takes a lot of inspiration from those days and adds a splash of rosewater to give it a perfect floral note. (If you can't locate rosewater easily or don't like the flavor, it's just as delicious without it.) The big plus of the Dutch baby is the batter is so easy to throw together in a blender and pour directly into a skillet. It's so much easier than making individual pancakes, and everyone gets to eat all at once!

1. Preheat the oven to 400°F.
2. Make the compote: Toss the raspberries, sugar, rosewater, and lemon zest in a medium bowl. Set aside to macerate for 10 to 15 minutes.
3. Make the Dutch baby: Add the eggs, milk, flour, granulated sugar, and salt to a blender and blend on high speed for 1 minute until smooth.
4. Melt the butter in a 10- or 12-inch cast-iron skillet over medium heat. Let the butter foam and start to brown, about 2 minutes. Remove from the heat and pour the batter into the skillet. Dot the compote over the entire surface of the batter. Transfer to the oven and bake for 30 to 35 minutes, until the Dutch baby rises up the sides of the skillet. Remove from the oven, finish with the lemon juice, dust with the powdered sugar, and serve immediately.

Serves 4

For the compote:
6 ounces fresh raspberries
¼ cup granulated sugar
¼ cup rosewater
Zest of 1 lemon

For the Dutch baby:
3 large eggs, room temperature
¾ cup whole milk, room temperature
½ cup all-purpose flour
2 tablespoons granulated sugar
1 teaspoon kosher salt
3 tablespoons unsalted butter
Juice of ½ lemon
¼ cup powdered sugar

Za'atar Shakshuka

VG, GF, NF

Shakshuka has overtaken the Western world in the last few decades, mainly because it's so fast and easy. My version inverts the usual formula of a spiced tomato sauce and instead uses a spice paste with a little tomato to finish. Probably the shortest ingredient list ever, the eggs get fried in za'atar paste until they're just set and then dollops of spicy tomato jam give a sweet and intriguing twist to the expected tomatoey flavors.

Serves 4

1 cup Za'atar Paste (page 73) or store-bought za'atar paste

8 large eggs, at room temperature

Kosher salt

Spicy Tomato Jam (page 50), at room temperature, for serving

Add the za'atar paste to a 9-inch nonstick skillet over medium heat. When the za'atar is bubbling, reduce the heat to medium. Crack the eggs around the pan as evenly spaced as possible. Reduce the heat to low and cook for 10 to 12 minutes, rotating the skillet every few minutes so the eggs cook evenly. Once the whites are set, remove from the heat and let sit for about 1 more minute to allow the eggs to settle. Season with a pinch of salt. Serve immediately with tomato jam.

Chocolate Tahini Overnight Oats

(V, GF, NF)

I came up with this recipe when I was hired to cater a Victoria's Secret shoot. The models needed a breakfast that was gluten-free and vegan. I wanted to offer them something delicious, healthy, and nourishing. This got the immediate stamp of approval from the Angels and has been a huge seller at the Grocer since day one. It's great for meal prep: make a big batch Sunday night, and you can portion it out all week for a no-effort breakfast that will fuel you all day.

Serves 6

2 cups extra-creamy oat milk

½ cup tahini

¼ cup date molasses

1 tablespoon cocoa powder

1 teaspoon kosher salt

2½ cups old-fashioned rolled oats

½ cup white sesame seeds

2 tablespoons chia seeds

Chopped pistachios and fresh fruit, for serving

Add the oat milk, tahini, date molasses, cocoa powder, and salt to a blender. Blend on high speed for about 2 minutes or until fully combined. In a large bowl, mix the oats, sesame seeds, and chia seeds. Pour the milk mixture over the oats and stir until fully combined. Cover and soak the oats overnight in the refrigerator for a porridge-like consistency. Divide among bowls and serve with chopped pistachios and fresh fruit or the topping of your choice.

Tomato Halloumi Skillet

VG, GF, NF

Halloumi, a firm and squeaky cheese popular in the Mediterranean, is delicious on its own, but it's transcendent after a quick sear. The dense texture of halloumi lets it stand up to high temps without melting. This recipe takes it to a whole other level by searing the halloumi in za'atar paste and spicy tomato jam for a sweet, nutty, spicy, savory, and salty combo that's entirely unique.

Add the za'atar paste to a medium nonstick skillet over medium heat. When it starts to sizzle, lay the slices of cheese around the skillet. Sear for 2 to 3 minutes on each side, until golden brown and crispy. Add the tomato jam and nigella seeds and shake the pan to evenly distribute. Cook for about 2 minutes more, until the tomato jam starts to bubble. Remove from the heat and serve immediately.

Serves 2

¼ cup Za'atar Paste (page 73) or store-bought za'atar paste

1 (8.8-ounce) halloumi cheese, drained and sliced

1 cup Spicy Tomato Jam (page 50) or store-bought marinara sauce

½ tablespoon nigella seeds

Aajeh, Lebanese Frittata

VG, GF, NF

As a kid, I used to go down to Samar's Bakery in my village and ask Samar to make aajeh for me, and she would bake it inside a dough, almost like a quiche. Because I didn't have her magic touch with dough, I adapted it into a naked frittata, so green and packed with flavor. The Greek yogurt and tomatoes help keep everything moist and soft, which means you can make it on Sunday and cut it into pieces to enjoy all week. Every time I make it, it reminds me so much of home.

Serves 4

Nonstick cooking spray

12 large eggs

¼ cup plain fat-free Greek yogurt

3 garlic cloves, grated

2 tablespoons extra-virgin olive oil

1 tablespoon kosher salt

1 tablespoon freshly ground black pepper

1 teaspoon Baharat (page 21) or ground cumin

4 packed cups fresh parsley leaves, chopped

5 scallions, sliced

1½ cups diced tomatoes (2 medium vine tomatoes)

1. Preheat the oven to 400°F. Coat a 10-inch cast-iron skillet with nonstick spray or rub with canola oil.

2. Add the eggs, yogurt, garlic, olive oil, salt, pepper, and baharat to a large bowl and whisk until fully combined. Fold in the parsley, scallions, and tomatoes. Pour the egg mixture into the prepared pan. Bake for 40 to 45 minutes, until the eggs are set all the way through. Remove from the oven and cool for about 10 minutes to let the frittata firm up. Serve from the skillet or run a butter knife around the edges to loosen, then set a plate on top of the pan. Flip everything over to release the frittata onto the plate. Serve immediately or refrigerate and serve cold.

BEC Everything Empanadas

NF

I came up with these empanadas during the early pandemic days when I was stuck at home and bored out of my mind. I had a lot of leftover hashweh in the freezer, so originally that was the meat. When I opened the Grocer, hungry New Yorkers demanded a classic BEC, so I subbed in bacon. But it's really the everything seasoning that makes these fluffy pockets of heaven so delicious, adding a roasty, salty, savory, spicy flavor.

1. Preheat the oven to 450°F. Line a rimmed baking sheet with parchment paper.
2. Make the filling: Arrange the bacon on the prepared baking sheet. Bake for about 12 minutes, until very crispy. Keep the oven on (you'll be using it later to bake the empanadas!), and remove the bacon to a plate to cool. Pour off the bacon fat and reserve 2 tablespoons. Add the eggs, yogurt, and pepper to a large bowl and whisk until fully combined.
3. Add the reserved bacon fat to a medium sauté pan over medium heat. When the fat is shimmering, pour in the egg mixture. Use a rubber spatula to stir and scrape the sides of the pan, working it into a soft scramble, 6 to 8 minutes. Remove the eggs to a large bowl and add the cheese. Crumble in the bacon and fold everything together. Let cool completely, about 30 minutes.
4. Line another rimmed baking sheet with parchment paper.
5. Make the empanadas: Arrange the empanada discs on the baking sheet. Scoop 2 tablespoons of cooled filling onto one side of the disc, then fold over to close. Use a fork to crimp and seal the edges shut. Brush the top of the empanada with vegetable oil and sprinkle with everything seasoning. Repeat with the remaining discs, filling, oil, and seasoning. (Any leftover filling makes a great snack!) Bake for about 10 minutes, until golden brown and flaky. Serve hot with spicy tomato jam.

> **Edy's Tips:** *If you can't find empanada discs, use premade pie crust and cut into 5-inch circles. Freeze the filled empanadas on a baking sheet until solid. Transfer to a zip-top bag and store in the freezer for up to 2 months. Add 4 to 5 minutes to the baking time.*

Makes 12 empanadas

For the filling:
8 ounces thick-cut bacon
10 large eggs
½ cup plain fat-free Greek yogurt
½ tablespoon freshly ground black pepper
2 tablespoons reserved bacon fat (or vegetable oil)
8 ounces cheddar cheese, shredded

For the empanadas:
12 (5-inch) empanada discs, thawed
½ cup vegetable oil, plus more as needed
⅓ cup Edy's Everything Seasoning (page 23) or store-bought everything bagel seasoning
Spicy Tomato Jam (page 50), for serving

3

Mix & Match

**Your Favorite
Neighborhood
Lunch Combo**

Salad

Summery Fattoush Salad

Fattoush is normally made with chopped lettuce, but it can get limp and lifeless fast. I like to lean toward a chunkier version with big, bold, crunchy vegetables in a large dice for that true summer feeling. While the vegetables are open to interpretation, the two key things that define a fattoush salad are the pita chips and the dressing. These dukkah pita chips add a little something unexpected to the mix, but it's really the sumac dressing that carries the day with a tart, floral note that brings it all together.

Serves 4 to 6

5 heirloom tomatoes,
   cut into wedges
1 English cucumber, quartered
   and cut into 1-inch pieces
1 bunch radishes, thinly sliced
1 cup thinly sliced scallions
½ cup fresh mint leaves
1½ cups Tangy Sumac
   Vinaigrette (page 77)
1 cup Dukkah Pita Chips

Add the tomatoes, cucumber, radishes, scallions, and mint to a large bowl. Add the dressing and toss to combine. Garnish with the pita chips just before serving.

Dukkah Pita Chips

Makes 8 cups

1 (12-ounce) package white
   or whole wheat pita
½ cup Dukkah (page 22) or
   Za'atar (page 23), or store-
   bought
¼ cup extra-virgin olive oil
1 teaspoon kosher salt

1. Preheat the oven to 350°F. Line a rimmed baking sheet with parchment paper.
2. Use kitchen scissors to cut the pita into large squares, about 2 inches each. In a large bowl, whisk together the dukkah, olive oil, and salt. Add the pita pieces and toss until completely coated. Spread the pita evenly on the prepared baking sheet. Bake for 6 to 8 minutes, until golden brown and crisp.
3. Serve right away or cool completely on the baking sheet and store in an airtight container at room temperature for up to 5 days.

Charred Corn, Tomato & Halloumi Salad

VG, GF, NF

This salad was born during my backyard dinner series, and it's the most seasonal, summery salad I could possibly imagine. It sings of summer all year long, but it's really worth waiting until produce hits its peak. When the corn is juicy and lightly charred and the tomatoes are sweet and plump, accented by the salty brine of halloumi, there is really nothing like it.

1. Preheat the oven to 400°F.
2. Char the corn and scallions over an open flame on your stovetop (or over high heat on a grill), making sure to rotate every minute or so for an even char, 3 to 5 minutes. Remove the scallions and chop into 2-inch pieces. Transfer the corn to a rimmed baking sheet and bake for 10 to 15 minutes, until plump and cooked through. Cool the corn for about 15 minutes, until cool enough to handle. Set a medium bowl on a towel to hold it in place. Set a corn cob upright in the bowl and run a knife down the sides to cut off the kernels. Repeat with the other cobs.
3. Heat the olive oil in a medium nonstick skillet over medium heat. When the oil is shimmering, add the cheese in a single layer. Sear for about 2 minutes on each side, until golden brown.
4. Add the tomatoes to a large bowl, along with the corn, scallions, cheese, ½ cup of the vinaigrette, and the salt. Toss to combine, then add the remaining vinaigrette to taste. Top with the nigella seeds before serving.

Serves 4 to 6

4 ears corn

7 scallions, cut into 2-inch pieces

1 tablespoon extra-virgin olive oil

1 (8.8-ounce) block halloumi cheese, drained and sliced into 6 pieces

4 heirloom tomatoes, quartered

1 cup Minty Vinaigrette (page 77)

1 teaspoon kosher salt

1 teaspoon nigella seeds

Watermelon Salad

VG, GF, NF

Watermelon has always been my favorite fruit, no competition. But I always thought of it as exclusively sweet. Years ago, when I was traveling in Bali, I had a watermelon salad loaded with lime, sesame oil, and shrimp that knocked my socks off. It opened a whole new world of possibility to me, which is honestly the best part of exploring the world. This recipe shows off watermelon's savory side through a very Lebanese lens: with tangy sumac, salty feta, and nutty chickpeas.

Serves 4 to 6

3 tablespoons extra-virgin olive oil

3 tablespoons fresh lime juice

2 tablespoons apple cider vinegar

3 tablespoons sumac

1 tablespoon freshly ground black pepper

2 (15.5-ounce) cans chickpeas, drained and rinsed

About 7 pounds watermelon, rind removed, and cut into 1-inch cubes

8 ounces feta cheese, crumbled

1 cup roughly chopped fresh cilantro

½ cup thinly sliced scallions

Whisk the olive oil, lime juice, vinegar, sumac, and black pepper in a large bowl. Add the chickpeas and toss. Add the watermelon, cheese, cilantro, and scallions and gently toss to combine. Serve immediately.

Edy's Tip: *The flavors improve as the salad sits, so make it up to 1 day ahead, store in the fridge, and add the last three ingredients just before serving.*

Butternut Squash Kale Salad

V, GF

This was a salad I first started making when I was catering sit-down dinners, coincidentally the same time that kale's popularity was reaching a fever pitch. This salad screams fall with hearty butternut squash roasted in date molasses (maple syrup is equally delicious!), buttery cashews, and kale covered in the creamy richness of a tahini dressing. The final touch, a sprinkling of pomegranate seeds, adds beautiful color and a burst of acidity to balance it all out.

1. Preheat the oven to 450°F. Line a rimmed baking sheet with parchment paper.

2. Make the squash: Arrange the squash on the prepared baking sheet. Whisk the date molasses, olive oil, cumin seeds, salt, and Aleppo pepper in a medium bowl, then pour over the squash. Toss to coat thoroughly. Roast for 30 to 35 minutes, until golden brown and tender. Remove from the oven and let cool completely, about 30 minutes.

3. Make the salad: In a large serving bowl, add the baby kale, cashews, pomegranate seeds, and squash. Drizzle in the dressing, toss well, and serve.

Serves 4 to 6

For the squash:

1 butternut squash (about 2 pounds), peeled, halved, seeded, and cut into 2-inch cubes

¼ cup date molasses

2 tablespoons extra-virgin olive oil

2 tablespoons cumin seeds

1 tablespoon kosher salt

1 tablespoon Aleppo pepper

For the salad:

8 ounces baby kale

1 cup roasted, salted cashews

¼ cup pomegranate seeds

¼ cup Spicy Tahini (page 76) or Cilantro Lime Tahini (page 76)

Tahini Caesar Salad

P, NF

When I opened the Grocer, I dreamed of doing a pop-up dinner series, but had to wait until the pandemic cooled down enough to safely gather indoors. The first one finally came on Valentine's Day 2021, a collaboration with my friend and fellow chef Bill Clark. This salad is a dreamed-up combination of his classic American cooking and my Lebanese influence: a reinvention of one of the best salads ever invented.

Serves 4 to 6

3 hearts of romaine, leaves separated

2 cups sugar snap peas, sliced

1 (8.8-ounce) block halloumi cheese, drained and shredded

1½ cups Caesar Tahini Dressing (page 76)

1 cup Sesame Aleppo Breadcrumbs (page 74)

Add the romaine, snap peas, cheese, and dressing to a large bowl. Toss to combine and top with the breadcrumbs before serving.

Kale Tabbouleh

V, NF

This was the first salad on the menu at the Grocer and, surprisingly, it got a lot of hate. So I'll just get this out of the way: This is not your grandmother's tabbouleh! No one has time to chop up a mountain of parsley. Kale is easier to prepare, holds up better, and adds a great texture. (There's still parsley in here too—don't panic.) I also swapped out bulgur for pearl couscous to give the salad a little more oomph and tossed it in a zippy lemon vinaigrette. A perfectly modern classic!

1. Add 10 cups water and the salt to a large saucepan. Bring to a boil over high heat. Stir in the couscous and cook for 7 to 9 minutes, until tender. Drain and rinse with cold water to cool.
2. Add the kale to a large bowl with ½ cup of the vinaigrette. Massage the kale to thoroughly incorporate the dressing. Add the tomatoes, cucumber, scallions, parsley, couscous, dukkah, and remaining ½ cup vinaigrette. Toss to combine and serve immediately.

Serves 4 to 6

2 tablespoons kosher salt

1 cup dried pearl couscous

2 bunches kale, stems removed, thinly sliced (10 to 12 cups)

1 cup Lemon Vinaigrette (page 77)

2 vine tomatoes, diced (2 cups)

1 cucumber, seeded and diced (2 cups)

1 bunch scallions, thinly sliced (2 cups)

2 bunches parsley with tender stems, finely chopped

½ cup Dukkah (page 22)

Toss the salad without the vinaigrette and it will stay good for up to 3 days in the fridge—great to pack for lunch with dressing on the side.

Edy's Tip

Soup

Lemony Chicken Orzo Soup

This soup is my whole childhood in a bowl. My Teita Odette was always making homemade chicken broth and, during the windy winters in Lebanon, this soup warmed me right up. It's become a signature recipe of the Grocer, getting lots of write-ups and shoutouts as the best chicken soup. Every time I smell it simmering on the stove, I'm transported back to the warm comfort of my grandmother's kitchen.

Serves 6 to 8

½ cup extra-virgin olive oil

3 medium yellow onions, diced (4 cups)

3 medium carrots, diced (2 cups)

4 celery stalks, diced (2 cups)

5 tablespoons kosher salt, plus more to taste

8 cups low-sodium chicken stock

5 bay leaves

1 tablespoon whole black peppercorns

8 ounces dried orzo

1 rotisserie chicken, skin removed and meat shredded

½ cup fresh lemon juice, from about 3 lemons

Chopped fresh parsley, for serving

1. Heat the olive oil in a large Dutch oven over medium heat. When the oil is shimmering, add the onions and sauté until translucent, about 8 minutes. Add the carrots and sauté for another 5 minutes, or until vibrantly colored. Add the celery and sauté for about 5 more minutes, until translucent. Season the vegetables with 1 tablespoon of the salt. Add the stock, 4 cups water, the bay leaves, black peppercorns, and the remaining 4 tablespoons salt. Simmer for 20 to 30 minutes, until the vegetables are soft.

2. Meanwhile, bring a large saucepan of salted water to a boil. Cook the orzo according to package directions for al dente. Drain and rinse under cold water to stop the cooking.

3. Add the rotisserie chicken to the soup and simmer for 5 minutes to warm through. Remove from the heat, stir in the lemon juice, and taste for seasoning. Scoop ¼ cup of the cooked orzo into each bowl, ladle the soup on top, and garnish with parsley. Serve immediately.

Moroccan Harissa Minestrone

V, NF

Harissa is a Moroccan chili paste that is used in Lebanon as a meat rub or a fiery accent in stews. During my time cooking in Italy, I made a lot of zuppa with spare pieces of vegetables and bits of leftover pasta. This soup strongly reminds me of the flavors of both places that formed my culinary identity. Historically, minestrone was the food of the poor, made with whatever was on hand, and it's still a great way to reduce food waste. Save your scraps in the freezer to make a homemade stock for later, and if you have veggies dying in the fridge, throw them in!

1. Make the soup: Heat the olive oil in a large Dutch oven over medium heat. When the oil is shimmering, add the onions and sauté, stirring often, until translucent, about 8 minutes. Add the carrots and sauté for another 5 minutes, until vibrant. Add the bell peppers and sauté for 5 more minutes, until tender. Add the celery and sauté for 5 more minutes, until translucent. Add the tomatoes, stock, harissa, salt, bay leaves, and 4 cups water. Simmer for 25 to 30 minutes, until the vegetables are soft. Stir in the chickpeas and simmer for 10 to 15 minutes, until soft. Add the parsley and lime juice and taste for seasoning. Keep warm over low heat.

2. Meanwhile, bring a large saucepan of salted water to a boil. Stir in the couscous and cook for 7 to 9 minutes, until tender. Drain and rinse with cold water to cool. Scoop ¼ cup of the couscous into each bowl and ladle the soup on top. Serve immediately.

Edy's Tip: *You can make this with finer couscous or keep it gluten-free with no couscous at all. The vegetables here are my standard base for this soup, but swap in anything you have in the crisper drawer (or freezer) that needs to get used up!*

Serves 6 to 8

For the soup:

¼ cup extra-virgin olive oil

2 medium yellow onions, diced (2 cups)

2 carrots, diced (2 cups)

2 red bell peppers, diced (2 cups)

4 celery stalks, diced (2 cups)

1 (28-ounce) can diced tomatoes

4 cups low-sodium vegetable stock

¼ cup harissa paste

3 tablespoons kosher salt, plus more

4 bay leaves

2 (15.5-ounce) cans chickpeas, drained and rinsed

2 tablespoons fresh or dried parsley

Juice of 1 lime

1 cup dried pearl couscous

Lemony Lentil Soup

V, GF, NF

Growing up, this was my favorite soup during Easter Lent. But adis bi hamod, as it's known in Arabic, is perfect year-round. Middle Eastern soups have a strong acidic streak, and the lemon is really on display here. To me, that's what makes a brothy soup so present and delicious. It's usually served chunky, but you can blend it if you want to for a smooth and creamy soup.

Serves 6 to 8

2 cups dried green lentils, rinsed and drained

6 bay leaves

5 tablespoons kosher salt

½ cup extra-virgin olive oil

3 medium yellow onions, sliced

2 pounds Yukon Gold potatoes, peeled and cubed

1 cup fresh lemon juice

1 bunch kale or Swiss chard, stems removed, chopped (about 4 cups)

1. Fill a large Dutch oven or pot with 4 quarts water and add the lentils, 3 bay leaves, and 2 tablespoons of the salt. Set over medium heat and simmer for 10 to 15 minutes, until al dente. Drain and discard the bay leaves.

2. Wipe out the Dutch oven and add the olive oil over medium-high heat. When the oil is shimmering, add the onions and sauté, stirring often, for 8 to 10 minutes, until soft. Add the potatoes and sauté for an additional 6 to 8 minutes, until lightly browned. Add 4 quarts water, the remaining 3 bay leaves, and the remaining 3 tablespoons salt. Bring to a simmer and cook for 10 to 15 minutes, until the potatoes are almost tender. Stir in the lentils and lemon juice and cook for an additional 10 minutes, or until the lentils and potatoes are soft. Remove from the heat and stir in the kale until wilted. Taste for seasoning and serve.

Make this with canned lentils, drained, for an even speedier soup.

Cumin, Carrot & Coconut Soup

V, GF, NF

I love to use coconut milk in soups, which is not at all Middle Eastern, but it adds a great creaminess. The fattiness of the coconut in this soup enhances all the flavors. I hate to say it, but most carrots in the US are not very flavorful. In Lebanon, the carrots seem like a whole different vegetable—they're so creamy and sweet. But a good roast and a gentle simmer help draw out an intense carroty flavor that makes this soup really come to life.

Serves 6 to 8

1. Preheat the oven to 400°F. Line a rimmed baking sheet with parchment paper.

2. Arrange the carrots on the prepared baking sheet and toss with 2 tablespoons of the olive oil, 1 tablespoon of the salt, and the cumin seeds. Roast for about 15 minutes, until fork tender.

3. Heat the remaining 3 tablespoons olive oil in a large Dutch oven over medium heat. Add the onions and garlic and sauté, stirring occasionally, until softened, 7 to 10 minutes.

4. Add the roasted carrots and any accumulated liquids, plus the coconut milk, vegetable stock, ground cumin, and remaining 2 tablespoons of salt to the pot. Stir to combine, bring to a simmer, and cook for 15 to 20 minutes, until the carrots are very soft. Turn off the heat and let cool for 5 minutes. Use an immersion blender or add to a blender in batches and blend until completely smooth. Taste for seasoning and serve with a sprinkle of dukkah, if using.

14 medium carrots, diced (7 cups)

5 tablespoons extra-virgin olive oil

3 tablespoons kosher salt

1 tablespoon cumin seeds

2 medium yellow onions, diced (2 cups)

4 garlic cloves

2 (13.5-ounce) cans full-fat coconut milk

2 cups low-sodium vegetable stock

1 tablespoon ground cumin

Dukkah (page 22), for garnish (optional)

Spicy Roasted Garlic & Tomato Soup

(V, GF, NF)

This is classic comfort at its finest and always on the menu at the Grocer in the cold months. Roasted garlic is the winner here, adding an unexpected caramelized sweetness. I especially love it with Pitadillas (page 129) for dipping or a swirl of Za'atar Goat Cheese (page 64) for extra creaminess. It even doubles as an incredible tomato sauce. The longer you let this soup simmer, the better it gets, as the tomatoes continue to develop in flavor. Even better, make it a day ahead and chill overnight. By the time you reheat it, it'll be complex and perfect.

Serves 6 to 8

For the roasted garlic:

1 head garlic, unpeeled and top sliced off

1 tablespoon extra-virgin olive oil

Kosher salt

For the soup:

½ cup extra-virgin olive oil

3 medium yellow onions, diced (4 cups)

2 (28-ounce) cans whole tomatoes

1 (28-ounce) can crushed tomatoes

3 tablespoons kosher salt

1 tablespoon sugar

¼ cup Aleppo pepper

¼ cup dried oregano

1. Preheat the oven to 350°F.

2. Make the roasted garlic: Set the head of garlic, cut-side up, on a piece of aluminum foil. Drizzle the olive oil over the top and season with a big pinch of salt. Wrap the foil tightly around the garlic and bake for 30 to 40 minutes, until golden brown. Set aside to cool.

3. Make the soup: Heat the olive oil in a large Dutch oven over medium heat. Add the onions and sauté, stirring often, until caramelized, 20 to 25 minutes. Add the whole and crushed tomatoes, then add a little water to each can to rinse out the remaining tomato and pour into the pot. Fill one can halfway with water and pour it into the pot. Stir and reduce the heat to low.

4. Unwrap the garlic and squeeze the cloves from their skin into the Dutch oven. Stir in the garlic, salt, sugar, Aleppo pepper, and oregano. Simmer on low heat for 1 to 2 hours, stirring every 30 minutes so the bottom doesn't scorch. Use an immersion blender or add to a blender in batches. Blend until completely smooth. Taste for seasoning and serve.

Sandwich
Za'atar Chicken Salad Sandwich

I started making this sandwich with leftover bits from chicken skewers, chopping it all up to come up with a chicken salad. Working in professional kitchens teaches you to never let food go to waste! I love to use yogurt instead of mayonnaise in all my cooking. Yogurt works overtime to keep things super moist, and the richness enhances the flavors while still adding a nice acidic tang. But more important, yogurt is a lighter and more refreshing alternative that doesn't leave you feeling overly full afterward.

Serves 6

1. Mix the yogurt, celery, capers, lemon juice, olive oil, and salt in a large bowl. Add the chicken and mix to coat. Chill in the refrigerator for at least 30 minutes or overnight.
2. Prepare the pita pockets by cutting a 2-inch slit at the top. Scoop a heaping ¼ cup chicken salad into each pita and add a few cucumber slices. Serve immediately.

2 cups fat-free Greek yogurt

3 celery stalks, diced (1 cup)

½ cup capers

¼ cup fresh lemon juice

1 tablespoon extra-virgin olive oil

1 tablespoon kosher salt

2 pounds Za'atar Chicken Thighs (page 145), diced

6 mini (4-inch) pita pockets

½ English cucumber, thinly sliced

Instead of Za'atar Chicken Thighs, you can use a shredded rotisserie chicken mixed with ¼ cup Za'atar Paste (page 73).

Edy's Tip

Crispy Mortadella Turkey Club

This is an ode to Maria, the patron saint of Edy's Grocer. When she still owned the store, then Maria's Deli, I used to swing by for her turkey sandwiches all the time. Her version was the best I had ever had, and during the pandemic I started to re-create it for myself at home. I added in crispy mortadella, an obsession I picked up while living in Italy—it lends a perfect accent to the classic flavors. This sandwich is not at the Grocer and will probably never show up on the menu. It's my secret treat that I only make for myself at home.

Serves 1

4 slices (4 ounces) pistachio mortadella

2 slices whole grain bread

2 tablespoons Spicy Tahini (page 76)

4 slices (4 ounces) roasted turkey

2 slices (2 ounces) pepper Jack cheese

Tomato slices, chopped lettuce, and pickles, for serving

1. Heat a large skillet over medium heat. Add the slices of mortadella and sear for about 2 minutes on each side, until browned and some fat has rendered. Remove to a paper towel to drain.

2. Add the slices of bread to the skillet and rub to coat in the fat. (If the mortadella is on the leaner side, add a little oil to the skillet.) Toast for about 2 minutes on each side, until golden brown. Remove to a plate and spread the spicy tahini on both slices. Stack the turkey, followed by the mortadella, cheese, tomato, lettuce, and pickles. Press on the top of the sandwich and cut in half before serving.

Pitadillas

During the times when Kivi, our nanny and family cook, was back in Sri Lanka visiting her family, my mom was left to her own devices in the kitchen. She has many talents, but cooking is not one of them, so we would eat a lot of khubz ou jebneh, which means bread and cheese, basically a Middle Eastern grilled cheese. She would use Armenian string cheese, which comes braided like a ponytail and soaked in brine, ready to be pulled apart and slowly melted. These pitadillas are my creative twist on Mom's specialty, pulling in some of the flavors I love the most.

Serves 4

Za'atar

VG, NF

1. Preheat the oven to 450°F. Line a rimmed baking sheet with parchment paper.
2. Whisk the olive oil, za'atar, and nigella seeds together in a medium bowl. Add the Armenian cheese, mozzarella cheese, and feta cheese to the bowl and mix until well combined.
3. Lay the lavash wraps flat and divide the cheese mixture along the bottom half of each wrap. Fold in half and press gently. Cut in half and transfer to the prepared baking sheet. Bake for 6 to 8 minutes, until the cheese is melted and the pitadilla is crispy.

¾ cup extra-virgin olive oil

½ cup Za'atar (page 23) or store-bought za'atar

1 tablespoon nigella seeds

12 ounces Armenian string cheese, shredded (2 cups)

12 ounces low-moisture mozzarella cheese, shredded (3 cups)

4 ounces feta cheese, crumbled

4 white or whole wheat lavash wraps or 12-inch flour tortillas

Pesto

VG

Follow the recipe, replacing the za'atar with 1 cup Greenery Pesto (page 73) or store-bought pesto.

Kimchi

VG, NF

Follow the recipe, replacing the za'atar with 1 pound vegan kimchi, drained and chopped.

Edy's Tip: *If you can't find Armenian string cheese, just up the amount of mozzarella.*

TO-GO
/5
0/4
3.50
1.50/5
pdates
w Us
Grocer
Refill
Pantry
Edy's grocer
Edy's

Toshka

Toshka is my favorite Syrian street food and was always the highlight of visiting my grandparents. The bread is extra crunchy, the meat is tender and perfectly seasoned, and the cheese is soft and gooey. In Syria, the sandwiches are grilled on a panini press. This version, fried in a skillet, is my own twist for all that crunchy, warm perfection.

1. In a small bowl, toss the Armenian cheese and mozzarella cheese together to combine. Divide the kafta mix into 8 equal balls. Heat a medium skillet over medium heat and brush lightly with olive oil.
2. Working one at a time, lay a lavash wrap flat and place a kafta ball in the center. Gently press the kafta with the heel of your palm to flatten until it covers the lavash. Lay in the skillet, meat-side down, and sear until the meat is browned, about 4 minutes. Flip so the meat in facing up and sprinkle ½ cup of the cheese mixture over the top. Fold in half and press gently. Toast for about 2 minutes, until nicely toasted on the bottom, then flip and toast for 2 more minutes. Continue with the remaining lavash, kafta, and cheese.
3. Serve the toshkas to order or arrange on a rimmed baking sheet and keep warm in a 200°F oven while making the rest. Slice the sandwiches in half and serve warm with a side of hummus, if using, for dipping.

Serves 8

12 ounces Armenian string cheese, shredded (2 cups)

4 ounces low-moisture mozzarella cheese, shredded (1 cup)

Kafta Mix (recipe follows)

Extra-virgin olive oil

8 white or whole wheat lavash wraps or 12-inch flour tortillas

Hummus, for serving (optional)

Kafta Mix

In a large bowl, use clean hands to mix the ground beef, onion, parsley, yogurt, baharat, and salt together. Cover tightly and refrigerate for up to 1 week or freeze for up to 3 months.

1 pound ground beef (preferably 90% lean)

1 small yellow onion, diced (½ cup)

½ cup chopped fresh parsley

2 tablespoons plain fat-free Greek yogurt

1 tablespoon Baharat (page 21)

1 tablespoon kosher salt

Chicken Shawarma Wrap

NF

You haven't lived until you've had a shawarma in Lebanon. It's my favorite street food, but there's a restaurant in Beirut called Za'atar w Zeit that makes the best one I've ever had. After a long night of clubbing, the freshly made lavash, tender chicken, extra toum, and briny pickles are the perfect thing to revive you, at least long enough to crawl into bed.

Serves 4

1 cup plain fat-free Greek yogurt

½ cup chopped fresh parsley leaves

¼ cup Toum (page 45) or 4 garlic cloves, grated

3 tablespoons Shawarma Seasoning (page 22)

2 tablespoons fresh lemon juice

2 tablespoon extra-virgin olive oil

1 rotisserie chicken, skin removed and meat shredded

4 white or whole wheat lavash wraps or 12-inch flour tortillas

1 vine tomato, halved and sliced (12 slices)

12 slices pickled turnips or other pickled vegetable (page 70)

2 heads romaine lettuce, thinly sliced

Any tahini sauce (page 76), for serving

1. Preheat the oven to 400°F. Line a rimmed baking sheet with parchment paper.

2. Whisk the yogurt, parsley, toum, shawarma seasoning, lemon juice, and olive oil together in a medium bowl. Fold in the chicken to fully coat.

3. Lay a lavash wrap flat and add 1 cup of the chicken mixture to the bottom half. Top with 3 tomato slices, 4 pickled turnip slices, and about ½ cup lettuce. Fold the sides over the filling, then roll tightly from the bottom up, like a burrito. Repeat with the other three sandwiches, then set the rolled sandwiches on the prepared baking sheet and bake for 6 to 8 minutes, until golden brown and crispy. (Alternatively, press in a panini press on medium heat for about 6 minutes.) Serve warm with tahini sauce for drizzling.

4

Easy, Breezy, Lemon Squeezy

Fast & Simple Weeknight Meals

Mujadara

V, GF, NF

When I was younger, the crispy onions and pools of labneh were my main attraction to mujadara. But when I was living on my own in New York and scraping by with low-paying jobs, I understood the dish in a whole new way. It's a cheap meal, basically a lentil porridge, that can be made in bulk and kept all week. I ended up eating it more often than not, and the warm seasonings made my new city feel like a real home at a tumultuous time in my life. The best part is it's actually better the longer it sits, as the flavors deepen as the days go by. It's still one of my favorite dishes to make when I need that extra hit of comfort.

Serves 4 to 6

For the mujadara:

1½ cups green lentils

1½ cups basmati rice

½ cup extra-virgin olive oil

3 medium yellow onions, sliced

2 tablespoons Baharat (page 21)

3 tablespoons kosher salt

5 bay leaves

Plain Labneh (page 55) or plain Greek yogurt, for serving (optional)

For the fried onions:

1 cup vegetable oil

2 medium yellow onions, halved and thinly sliced

Kosher salt

1. Make the mujadara: Add the lentils to a medium bowl. Fill the bowl with hot water to cover and let the lentils soak for about 20 minutes, until slightly tender to the touch. While the lentils are soaking, rinse and drain the rice until the water runs clear. Set aside to drain thoroughly. When the lentils are done, drain.

2. Add the olive oil to a large saucepan over medium heat. When the oil is shimmering, add the onions. Sauté, stirring occasionally, until the onions turn golden brown, 10 to 15 minutes. Stir in the lentils, rice, baharat, salt, and bay leaves. Sauté for 4 to 5 minutes, until the lentils and rice are coated and the mixture is fragrant. Add 4 cups water, 1 cup at a time, while stirring to incorporate. Cover and reduce the heat to low. Let the rice and lentils simmer until the water is absorbed, 20 to 25 minutes. Uncover and fluff the rice with a fork. Taste for seasoning.

3. Make the fried onions: While the lentils and rice are simmering, add the vegetable oil to a medium skillet over medium-high heat. When the oil is shimmering, add the onions and fry for 3 to 5 minutes, until crunchy and golden brown. Use a slotted spoon to transfer the fried onions to paper towels to drain. Season with a pinch of salt.

4. Divide the mujadara among bowls and serve with the fried onions and a dollop of labneh, if using.

Fasolia ou Riz

V, GF

Fasolia is an all-day affair. Made with dried beans and a lamb shank, it simmers for hours on the stove until the beans are buttery soft and delicious. This is my shortcut version of it, using canned beans and cutting out the meat to save time. But what it lacks in effort, it makes up for in flavor with a mix of spices and layers of seasoning that brings me back to the comfort food I love the most.

Serves 4 to 6

1 cup extra-virgin olive oil

3 medium yellow onions, halved and sliced

⅓ cup sliced garlic

2 tablespoons tomato paste

3 tablespoons kosher salt

2 tablespoons Baharat (page 21)

1 tablespoon smoked paprika

1 (28-ounce) can crushed tomatoes

1 (28-ounce) can diced tomatoes

6 to 8 bay leaves

2 cinnamon sticks

3 (15.5-ounce) cans red kidney beans, drained and rinsed

¼ cup toasted pine nuts, for garnish

Vermicelli Rice (page 153), for serving

Heat the olive oil in a large Dutch oven over medium heat. When the oil is simmering, add the onions and sauté for about 10 minutes, until translucent. Stir in the garlic and tomato paste and continue cooking, stirring occasionally, until the paste is dark red and the garlic is fragrant, 5 to 7 minutes. Stir in the salt, baharat, and paprika and cook for about 5 minutes, until the onions are caramelized. Add the crushed tomatoes, diced tomatoes, bay leaves, and cinnamon sticks and simmer for about 15 minutes to let the flavors meld. Finally, add the beans and simmer for 25 to 30 minutes, until the stew thickens. Taste for seasoning and remove the cinnamon and bay leaves. Garnish with the pine nuts and serve with vermicelli rice.

To Paola

If you were wondering where I got my entrepreneurial side, it would be from my mother, Paola, or Mam, as I would call her. She grew up in war-torn Lebanon and at age fifteen was sent off to Geneva for school. After marrying my father, Simon, whom she met in Anfeh, they settled in the village and she became a true force. In 1992, she opened her own beauty salon, Institut Paola, and made waves with the modern hairstyles, jewelry, bags, and makeup that she sold. Her salon was booked months in advance, and women from surrounding towns and cities would flock to Anfeh to see the latest arrivals.

Running a small business was different before the internet and social media, but Paola had the "it" factor and knew how to talk anyone into buying a product. As a child, I would sit on a chair by the register and watch her lean over the glass display case, pulling jewelry, makeup, and perfume for women hungry to feel beautiful. She made every woman who stepped into her space feel seen and heard, like therapy in salon time. The ladies came in and out, kissing cheeks, sipping on Turkish coffee, biting into cookies, all the while swearing that *they never eat sugar these days*. The soft pink and purple couches that surrounded the waiting room were packed with gossip and secrets, and I absorbed everything, my eyes wide with wonder. This was a new generation of women with their eyes on the Western world, something my grandmothers could never understand.

While juggling her family and a successful business, Mam somehow made it a daily practice for us to sit together around the table and enjoy a meal as a family. In Lebanon, the most important meal of the day is lunch. My sister and I would get home from school and Mam and Pap would be there, ready to eat lunch together. When we moved to America, this practice continued over dinner every night. Being united as a family, sharing a meal, and checking in not only made me feel safe in our new home but also made me feel cherished, loved, and cared for.

For all our similarities in our entrepreneurial streak, we ironically have one big difference: Paola may be a great businesswoman, but she's hopeless in the kitchen. (The irony that she spent her life running hair salons and I was bald by age twenty-two also should be mentioned.) But Mam had one dish up her sleeve, and she did it very well. She learned to make émincé de poulet in Geneva while attending college. It's quick and easy and was the only thing she knew how to make from scratch. Even though it's not Lebanese, this creamy curry chicken stew immediately transports me back to her. When I make this dish, no matter where I am, I feel the same love and care I felt as a young child, sitting down at the table with those I cherish the most: my family.

Émincé de Poulet

NF

1. Add 2 tablespoons of the butter and 2 tablespoons of the olive oil to a Dutch oven over medium heat. When the butter is melted, add the shiitake mushrooms and a good pinch of salt. Sauté, stirring occasionally, until browned, 10 to 12 minutes. Remove the mushrooms to a plate and repeat with the remaining 2 tablespoons butter and oil and the baby bella mushrooms, seasoning with another pinch of salt.

2. While the mushrooms cook, add the chicken to a medium bowl and toss with the flour, 1 tablespoon of the curry powder, 1 tablespoon of the salt, and the pepper. When the mushrooms are done, add 2 tablespoons of the vegetable oil to the Dutch oven over medium-high heat. Sear half of the chicken in the oil, about 4 minutes on each side. Remove to the same plate as the mushrooms. Repeat with the remaining vegetable oil and chicken. Add all of the chicken and mushrooms back to the Dutch oven. Stir in the chicken stock and remaining 1 tablespoon curry powder and 1 tablespoon salt. Simmer for about 15 minutes, until the sauce is thickened and slightly reduced. Reduce the heat to medium-low and add the heavy cream. Continue simmering for 6 to 8 more minutes, being careful not to let it boil, until the sauce is silky and warmed through. Serve immediately with parsley and vermicelli rice.

Serves 4 to 6

4 tablespoons unsalted butter

4 tablespoons extra-virgin olive oil

7 ounces shiitake mushrooms, sliced

2 tablespoons kosher salt, plus more as needed

1 pound baby bella mushrooms, sliced

3 pounds boneless, skinless chicken breasts, cut into 2-inch cubes

2 tablespoons all-purpose flour

2 tablespoons curry powder

1 tablespoon freshly ground black pepper, plus more for serving

4 tablespoons vegetable oil

3 cups low-sodium chicken stock

1½ cups heavy cream

Roughly chopped fresh parsley, for serving

Vermicelli Rice (page 153), for serving

Lemony Sheet Pan Chicken

GF, NF

Growing up, I always looked forward to coming home to this meal when Kivi, our nanny and cook, made it. I could smell it cooking from the doorway and my heart would beat faster in anticipation. Her version was made in a casserole dish with a lemon sauce and a low and slow bake until rich and tender. This is my version, an easy weeknight shortcut that bakes all on one sheet pan in an hour. With a side of vermicelli rice, this is still a dish that gets my heart racing.

Serves 4 to 6

½ cup fresh lemon juice

2 lemons, zested and sliced into ½-inch rounds

¾ cup extra-virgin olive oil

6 garlic cloves, grated

1 bunch thyme sprigs

5 rosemary sprigs

5 bay leaves

1 tablespoon dried oregano

2 tablespoons kosher salt

1 teaspoon freshly ground black pepper

1 pound Yukon Gold potatoes, sliced into ½-inch rounds

2 pounds boneless, skinless chicken thighs

1 medium yellow onion, sliced into ½-inch rounds

1. Preheat the oven to 400°F.
2. Whisk the lemon juice, lemon zest, olive oil, garlic, thyme, rosemary, bay leaves, oregano, salt, and pepper in a large bowl.
3. Arrange the potato slices on a rimmed baking sheet. Drizzle ¼ cup of the lemon sauce over the top and toss to coat. Bake for 10 minutes, or until the potatoes are slightly tender.
4. While the potatoes bake, add the chicken, onion, and lemon slices to the remaining lemon sauce and toss to coat. At the 10-minute mark, remove the baking sheet from the oven and flip the potatoes. Arrange the chicken, onion, and lemon slices over the baking sheet with the potatoes and drizzle any remaining dressing over the top. Return to the oven and bake for 45 to 50 minutes, until the chicken is golden brown and cooked through (165°F to 170°F on an instant-read thermometer). Serve immediately.

Za'atar Chicken Thighs

GF, NF

This dish is my favorite protein (chicken) with my favorite seasonings (sumac and za'atar). It might be the purest expression of me in this book. It's always been a big hit at my backyard dinners and an even bigger hit at the weddings I've catered. The spice rub perfectly penetrates the chicken flesh, giving it lots of flavor and plenty of moisture. The bonus cucumber slaw on top is refreshing and herbaceous and pulls everything together. Any leftovers can be made into a Za'atar Chicken Salad Sandwich (page 125) the next day!

1. Make the chicken: Add the za'atar, sumac, olive oil, lemon juice, oregano, salt, and garlic to a large bowl. Whisk to combine. Add the chicken thighs to the bowl and toss to coat thoroughly. Cover with plastic wrap and marinate in the refrigerator for at least 30 minutes or up to 24 hours.

2. Preheat the oven to 450°F. Line a rimmed baking sheet with parchment paper and set a wire rack on top. Spray the rack with nonstick cooking spray.

3. Remove the chicken from the marinade, letting the excess drip off, and arrange on the prepared rack. (The baking sheet will catch all the drippings and the rack will allow hot air to flow all around the thighs for even baking.) Roast in the oven for 16 to 18 minutes, until cooked through. Remove from the oven, lightly tent with foil, and set aside to rest for 8 minutes.

4. While the chicken is resting, make the slaw: Add the cucumber, mint, lemon juice, olive oil, and salt to a medium bowl and toss to combine.

5. When the chicken is rested, divide among plates and pile the slaw on top of the chicken. Serve with a lemon wedge for squeezing.

Serves 4 to 6

For the chicken:

¼ cup Za'atar (page 23) or store-bought

¼ cup sumac

¼ cup extra-virgin olive oil

¼ cup fresh lemon juice

2 tablespoons dried oregano

2 tablespoons kosher salt

4 garlic cloves, grated

4 pounds boneless, skinless chicken thighs

Nonstick cooking spray

Lemon wedges, for serving

For the slaw:

1 English cucumber, peeled into long ribbons

¼ cup fresh mint leaves, chopped

1 tablespoon fresh lemon juice

1 tablespoon extra-virgin olive oil

Pinch of kosher salt

Edy's Tip: You can grill the chicken instead of roasting it. Prepare a grill for medium heat and grill for about 8 minutes on each side.

Everything Sumac Salmon

P, GF, NF

This is the number one easy weeknight meal that I make at home when I want something fast. It's simple but complex in flavor. The sumac adds a citrusy note, the everything seasoning adds a salty and nutty flavor, and the spicy tomato jam adds an amazing savory sweetness. Roasting salmon is almost impossible to mess up—just set a timer and enjoy a perfectly cooked fillet in minutes.

Serves 4 to 6

2 tablespoons extra-virgin olive oil

2 pounds salmon, cut into 4 to 6 fillets

2 tablespoons sumac

¼ cup Edy's Everything Seasoning (page 23) or store-bought everything bagel seasoning

1 cup Spicy Tomato Jam (page 50; optional)

1. Preheat the oven to 425°F. Line a rimmed baking sheet with parchment paper and drizzle with the olive oil.
2. Season the salmon fillets with the sumac and then the everything seasoning. Gently press to evenly distribute the spices on the fillets for a perfect crust. Transfer to the prepared baking sheet and bake for about 15 minutes, until the salmon is cooked through. Serve the salmon with tomato jam, if using.

Saffron & Lemon Cod

P, GF, NF

Saffron and fish are perfect together. Saffron has an intriguing flavor—a little sweet, a little bitter, and ultimately floral and fragrant. It's not cheap, but lucky for you, a little goes a long way. Especially with a delicate fish like cod, saffron really takes over and elevates the dish. Because this dish is so pared back, it's important to invest in really good fish here. Skip the plastic-wrapped stuff at the grocery store (which is perfect for stews or frying!) and head straight to the fish counter to get the freshest fillets possible. They should be firm and not at all fishy. It'll pay off big time when you take your first bite!

1. Preheat the oven to 450°F.
2. Pour the water into a small bowl. Gently crush the saffron with your fingers into the bowl. Bloom the saffron in the water for about 10 minutes—the water should be fragrant and fire red. Whisk in the olive oil, garlic, lemon zest and juice, salt, and pepper.
3. Arrange the cod fillets in a 9 by 13-inch baking dish and season with a good pinch of salt. Pour the saffron mixture over the fish. Immediately transfer to the oven and bake for about 15 minutes, until cooked through.
4. Divide the fish among plates and spoon the pan juices over the top. Serve with the fried nut mix, if using, to sprinkle on top.

Serves 4

½ cup boiling water
½ teaspoon saffron
½ cup extra-virgin olive oil
3 garlic cloves, grated
Zest and juice of 2 lemons
½ tablespoon kosher salt, plus more as neeed
1 teaspoon freshly ground black pepper
2 pounds cod, cut into 4 fillets
Fried Nut Mix (page 81), for serving (optional)

To Kivi

Growing up in Lebanon, my family was the typical nuclear unit of mom, dad, sister, and me, plus one extra special member: Kivi. She was my nanny, my confidante, my protector, and most of all, the executive chef of the Massih household. Kivi came to us in 1993 from Sri Lanka. She was in her forties and a mother of eight kids of her own back home. She was no more than five feet tall and her beautiful black hair went all the way down to her knees. While most adults and kids in my life tried to get me to act normal, Kivi allowed me to be myself. She would always chase me at birthday parties to make sure I was eating. She'd pamper me each morning by waking me up and putting my socks on my feet while I was still in bed, just so I wouldn't get cold. I loved her coconut oil smell and her dry, pink palms, and I often wondered how a fearless, strong woman like Kivi was living in my little village of Anfeh, watching over my sister and me.

I always wanted to be in the kitchen helping, and where most adults would shoo me away, Kivi welcomed me in. Kivi entered our kitchen as a human encyclopedia of cooking techniques, so it was only a matter of time until she learned and perfected all the recipes from both of my grandmothers, Odette and Jacqueline. She captivated me the most when she was in her element cooking in the kitchen. As a toddler, I'd sit on the black marble kitchen counter, snack in hand, and watch her prepare meals so gracefully and deliberately, like a dancer. I loved most of all when she made her famous bazella ou riz with vermicelli rice.

Kivi would make a big batch of kafta, forming it into patties and balls, some for now and some for the freezer, just like Jacquo taught her. Wetting her hands with oily water to make perfect kafta meatballs, she would sear the balls in our large red pot, then add the tomato sauce, seasoning, bay leaves, and a bag of frozen peas and carrots. While the kafta was simmering, she fried vermicelli noodles in a sizzling pot slicked with oil. She stirred in the rice, water, salt, and bay leaves. Then she alternated between setting the table, rotating the rice pot, and stirring the meatball stew, making sure not to scorch the bottom of the pot. She proudly presented her fluffy white rice with little brown vermicelli noodles sprinkled in, and the bubbling deep red edges of the pot with meatball stew with little peas and carrots floating. My sister and I would run into the kitchen with our bowls, waiting to be served.

The way she protected me, and let me be who I am, helped me shape my identity at such a young age. When I step into the kitchen—any kitchen, whether it's the Grocer or a client's house—I try to always remember the grace Kivi carried herself with in a foreign place, while cooking from her heart no matter what and who was around her. I remind myself to embody Kivi, stay confident, be who I truly am, and never let go of my values. Starting my own little community at the Grocer through pop-up dinners, fundraisers, and just spreading the joy of Lebanese cooking has made me shed the fear of being a foreigner and instead raised a sense of belonging in my little corner of Greenpoint, Brooklyn.

Bazella ou Riz

GF, NF

1. Scoop and roll the kafta into small balls, about 1 tablespoon each, yielding 28 to 30 meatballs.

2. Heat the vegetable oil in a large Dutch oven over medium-high heat. When the oil is shimmering, add the meatballs in batches and use tongs to rotate and sear until browned on all sides, 4 to 5 minutes total. Add the tomato sauce, chicken stock, baharat, salt, and pepper to the meatballs. Reduce the heat to medium-low and simmer for 8 to 12 minutes, stirring often, until incorporated and the sauce begins to thicken. Stir in the frozen vegetables and continue simmering for 6 to 8 minutes, letting the sauce reduce slightly and develop in flavor. Taste for seasoning before serving over vermicelli rice.

Serves 4

1 pound Kafta Mix (page 131)

2 tablespoons vegetable oil

4 cups Edy's Tomato Sauce (page 180), or store-bought marinara

1 cup low-sodium chicken stock

1 tablespoon Baharat (page 21)

1 tablespoon kosher salt

2 teaspoons freshly ground black pepper

1 pound frozen pea and carrot mix

Vermicelli Rice (page 153), for serving

Sides

Vermicelli Rice

V, NF

This is my go-to starchy base that has soaked up all the saucy dishes in my life. When I moved to America, I was introduced to Rice-A-Roni, a delicious, dumbed-down version, but nothing will ever replace my homemade vermicelli rice. It's a must-have almost every time I sit down to eat. It gives me a little thrill every time I start frying the noodles, as I'm transported back home.

Add the vegetable oil to a medium saucepan over medium heat. When the oil is shimmering, add the vermicelli noodles. Sauté, stirring often, until the noodles turn golden brown, about 8 minutes. Stir in the rice and add the salt, bay leaves, and 4½ cups water. Mix well, bring to a simmer, then cover and reduce the heat to low. Simmer for 10 minutes, then rotate the pot 90 degrees and simmer for about 10 more minutes, until the rice and noodles are cooked through. Remove from the heat and use a fork to fluff the rice. Cover and steam for 10 more minutes, until the rice is swollen. Serve immediately.

Serves 4 to 6

½ cup vegetable oil

4 ounces vermicelli noodles or angel hair pasta, broken into small pieces

2 cups jasmine rice, rinsed and drained

1½ tablespoons kosher salt

5 to 6 bay leaves

Harissa Lime Brussels Sprouts

V, GF, NF

I had never seen Brussels sprouts before coming to the US. They weren't in Lebanon and were some of the only produce that was brand-new to me. I immediately thought they were so cute! When I worked my first restaurant job in New York, I would flash-fry Brussels sprouts and toss them in harissa and lime. They're roasted here, but otherwise this sticks pretty close to that dish because honestly it was a perfect pairing of flavors.

1. Preheat the oven to 400°F.
2. Whisk the harissa paste, herby harissa, lime zest and juice, olive oil, and salt in a large bowl. Add the Brussels sprouts and toss to coat. Spread out on a rimmed baking sheet and transfer to the oven. Roast for 16 to 18 minutes, until golden brown, or up to 20 minutes for an extra-crispy sprout. Transfer to a bowl and serve immediately.

Serves 4 to 6

1 tablespoon harissa paste

1 tablespoon Herby Harissa Seasoning (page 23; optional)

Zest and juice of 2 limes

2 tablespoons extra-virgin olive oil

1 tablespoon kosher salt

1½ pounds Brussels sprouts, trimmed and halved

Sweetie Tahini Eggplant

(VG, GF, NF)

It's hard to say if I love eggplant or if I had no choice but to love it, since my Teita Odette made fried eggplant every other night. But when I started catering, I did a few test runs of roasted eggplant until it eventually became a permanent part of my menu. I came up with this at my parents' house in Boston in an impulsive stroke of genius. The mix of rich tahini, fresh herbs, bitingly sharp scallions, and salty feta plays perfectly against the meltingly soft flesh of the eggplant.

Serves 4 to 6

For the eggplant:

½ cup extra-virgin olive oil, plus more for drizzling

2 large eggplants, sliced into 1-inch-thick coins

1 tablespoon kosher salt

For the sauce:

1 cup Sweet Tahini (page 76)

3 scallions, thinly sliced

2 tablespoons chopped fresh parsley

2 tablespoons chopped fresh mint

5 ounces feta cheese

1. Preheat the oven to 450°F. Line a rimmed baking sheet with parchment paper and drizzle liberally with olive oil.

2. Make the eggplant: Place the eggplant slices on the tray, brush with the olive oil, and season with the salt. Roast in the oven for about 20 minutes, until soft.

3. While the eggplant is roasting, make the sauce: In a medium bowl, whisk the tahini sauce, scallions, 1 tablespoon parsley, and 1 tablespoon mint. Crumble in the feta and gently fold.

4. Transfer the roasted eggplant to a serving platter and spoon over the tahini feta sauce. Garnish with the remaining 1 tablespoon parsley and 1 tablespoon mint before serving.

Batata Harra

V, GF, NF

Mila has been my best friend for over a decade and has been with the Grocer since day one. She runs the kitchen, and her wisdom and patience have influenced every recipe in this book. After working together for so long, I finally got to bring her to Lebanon with me in the summer of 2022. It was the first time I brought someone from my new life into my old life. I was excited to be able to introduce her to the food I grew up with and to enable an old friend to understand me in a deeper way. While we were there, we became obsessed with ordering batata harra—meaning spicy potatoes, a Lebanese take on potato hash—because potatoes are so good in Lebanon and every restaurant makes the dish completely different. This is our spin, and no matter how many times we make it, we never get sick of it.

1. Preheat the oven to 450°F. Line a rimmed baking sheet with parchment paper.
2. Make the potatoes: Whisk the garlic, lemon juice, olive oil, stock, salt, harissa paste, and tomato paste in a large bowl. Add the potatoes and toss to coat. Transfer the potatoes and sauce to the prepared baking sheet. Bake for 35 to 40 minutes, until the potatoes are fork tender and the liquid has mostly evaporated.
3. Make the fried capers: While the potatoes bake, add the olive oil and capers to a small saucepan over medium-high heat. When the capers start sizzling, fry for about 12 minutes, until crispy. Add the cilantro (step back, it can splatter) and fry for an additional minute, or until the cilantro is fragrant. Remove from the heat and let the oil cool while the potatoes finish.
4. Transfer the baked potatoes to a large serving platter and spoon the caper oil on top. Serve immediately.

Serves 4 to 6

For the potatoes:
4 garlic cloves, grated
½ cup fresh lemon juice
½ cup extra-virgin olive oil
½ cup low-sodium vegetable or chicken stock
2 tablespoons kosher salt
1 to 2 tablespoons harissa paste
1 tablespoon tomato paste
3 pounds Yukon Gold potatoes, cut into 1-inch cubes

For the fried capers:
½ cup extra-virgin olive oil
½ cup drained capers
2 cups roughly chopped fresh cilantro, leaves and tender stems

Hosting & Gathering

Yalla, Bring Your Friends, We're Having a Party!

Seasonal Couscous Salads

This salad started out as an orzo salad that I made for my backyard dinner parties. When I opened the Grocer, I was buying couscous in bulk and needed a place to put it all. (Can you tell being a small business owner has taught me to be more creative with what I have?) It turns out couscous was a better answer for the salad because it holds up longer without getting mushy and feels less heavy than orzo. It's a great blank canvas for seasonal vegetables, and you can feel free to play around with dressings depending on what you have on hand. This is one of the things that is constantly in my fridge, at the Grocer, and on my dinner table.

Serves 6 to 8

Fall/Winter

V, NF

1 butternut squash, peeled, halved, seeded, and cut into 1-inch pieces

¾ cup maple syrup

2 tablespoons extra-virgin olive oil

1 tablespoon Aleppo pepper

4 tablespoons kosher salt

3 cups dried pearl couscous (1 pound)

1 (15.5-ounce) can chickpeas, drained and rinsed

½ cup drained capers

½ cup thinly sliced scallions

1 cup any vinaigrette, store-bought or homemade (page 77)

1. Preheat the oven to 400°F. Line a rimmed baking sheet with parchment paper.

2. Toss the squash, ¼ cup of the maple syrup, the olive oil, Aleppo pepper, and 1 tablespoon of the salt on the prepared baking sheet. Roast for 20 to 25 minutes, until fork tender. Set aside to cool for about 30 minutes.

3. Bring a large pot of water to a boil over high heat. Stir in the remaining 3 tablespoons salt and the couscous. Cook according to the package directions to al dente. Drain and rinse under cold water to stop the cooking.

4. Transfer the couscous to a large bowl with the squash, chickpeas, capers, scallions, vinaigrette, and the remaining ½ cup maple syrup. Toss to mix well. Serve immediately or cover and refrigerate for up to 3 days.

Spring/Summer

1. Bring a large, wide pot of water to a boil over high heat. Stir in the salt. Add the corn cobs to the water and boil for 5 to 7 minutes, until the corn is plump and tender. Use tongs to remove the corn to a strainer, keeping the water boiling.

2. Add the couscous to the boiling water. Cook according to the package directions to al dente. Two minutes before the couscous is done, add the asparagus to blanch it. Drain the asparagus and couscous and rinse under cold water to stop the cooking.

3. Set a medium bowl on a towel to hold it in place. Set a corn cob upright in the bowl and run a knife down the sides to remove the kernels. Repeat with the other cobs.

4. Transfer the couscous and asparagus to a large bowl and add the cucumber, tomatoes, capers, corn, and vinaigrette. Toss to mix well. Serve immediately or cover and refrigerate for up to 3 days.

¼ cup kosher salt

3 ears corn

3 cups dried pearl couscous (1 pound)

1 bunch asparagus, bottoms trimmed, cut into 2-inch pieces

1 English cucumber, diced

8 ounces cherry tomatoes, halved

½ cup drained capers

1 cup any vinaigrette, store-bought or homemade (page 77)

Garlicky Potato Salad

VG, GF, NF

When I was growing up, we didn't eat mashed potatoes; instead this lemony, garlicky salad was our standard side dish. Greek yogurt makes it creamy and delicious, with a lighter touch than the mayonnaise in traditional American-style potato salad. The final touch of a bright and fresh herb dressing gives it a bold and colorful twist and makes it the perfect addition to any backyard cookout.

Serves 6 to 8

3 pounds Yukon Gold potatoes, peeled and cut into 2-inch pieces

Kosher salt

1 head plus 2 garlic cloves

½ cup plus 1 tablespoon extra-virgin olive oil

2 scallions, thinly sliced

1 cup chopped fresh parsley

½ preserved lemon, minced, or zest of 1 lemon

1 teaspoon cumin seeds

1 cup plain fat-free Greek yogurt

¼ cup fresh lemon juice

1. Preheat the oven to 450°F.

2. Add the potatoes and 3 big pinches of salt to a large pot. Add water to cover the potatoes and set over medium-high heat. Bring to a simmer, then lower the heat, cover, and cook for 30 to 35 minutes, until the potatoes are fork tender but still firm.

3. Meanwhile, slice the top off the head of garlic and set it on a piece of aluminum foil. Drizzle with 1 tablespoon of the olive oil and a big pinch of salt. Wrap the foil tightly around the garlic and bake for 20 minutes, or until golden brown.

4. Whisk the scallions, parsley, preserved lemon, cumin seeds, and ¼ cup of the olive oil in a medium bowl. In a separate medium bowl, squeeze the roasted garlic cloves from their skin. Use a whisk to mash the cloves into a thick paste, then add the Greek yogurt, lemon juice, and the remaining ¼ cup olive oil. Grate the remaining 2 garlic cloves into the bowl. Whisk until fully combined.

5. When the potatoes are ready, drain and rinse under cold water to stop the cooking. Transfer the potatoes to a large bowl and let cool for 10 minutes. Using a potato masher or ricer, mash the potatoes very well until smooth. Pour the yogurt mixture over the potatoes and mix well. Top with the herb dressing and serve warm or cover and refrigerate for up to 3 days and serve cold.

Spicy Fig & Pistachio Stuffins

Every year at the Grocer, we do a full Mediterranean Thanksgiving meal that customers can preorder and take home to share with their loved ones. When I came to the States and experienced my first Thanksgiving, stuffing was my immediate favorite dish. So I really wanted to re-create what I love about this classic American dish with a punch of Lebanese flavors. I love the spicy fig jam here, as it adds the perfect amount of sweetness, and the chopped pistachios give the tender dish a nutty crunch. But the best part of this recipe (in my humble opinion!) is that the stuffing is baked in a muffin tin (hence, stuffins), so it's already perfectly portioned out for guests (or a solo snack!) and every bite has crispy edges.

1. Preheat the oven to 425°F. Coat a 16-cup muffin tin with nonstick spray.
2. Heat the olive oil in a large skillet over medium heat. When the oil is shimmering, add the onion and celery. Sauté, stirring occasionally, until translucent, 6 to 8 minutes. Add the thyme, rosemary, 1 tablespoon of the salt, and the black pepper. Continue to sauté for 5 minutes. Reduce the heat to low and add the fig jam and stock. Stir to combine and simmer for 5 minutes, or until the vegetables are soft.
3. Add the cubed bread to a medium bowl. Pour the fig mixture over the top and stir well to combine. Let sit for about 10 minutes, until the bread fully absorbs the liquid. Add the pistachios and remaining 1 tablespoon salt and mix well. Divide the stuffing evenly among the muffin tin cups, pressing to compact it. Bake for 15 to 18 minutes, until golden brown all over. Cool completely in the tin, about 1 hour, and serve at room temperature.

Makes 16 stuffins

Nonstick cooking spray

2 tablespoons extra-virgin olive oil

1 medium yellow onion, finely chopped

6 celery stalks, diced

3 sprigs fresh thyme, stems removed

3 sprigs fresh rosemary, stems removed

2 tablespoons kosher salt

1 tablespoon freshly ground black pepper

1 cup Spicy Fig Jam (page 54) or store-bought fig jam

2 cups low-sodium vegetable or chicken stock

1 loaf crusty sourdough, cut into 1-inch cubes

1 cup pistachios, chopped

Edy's Tip: *Stuffins can be cooled and frozen in the muffin tin until solid. Transfer to a zip-top bag and store in the freezer for up to 2 months. Place back in the muffin tin and reheat in the oven at 425°F for about 10 minutes, until warmed through.*

Orzo Mac & Cheese

VG, NF

I first created this dish for a catering job at a child's birthday party. The mom wanted mac and cheese and I had a lot of orzo lying around, so I put two and two together and had an immediate crowd pleaser. In college, I hated making roux and bechamel, so I came up with an alternate sauce, what I like to call cheese ganache. It's as easy as pouring hot cream over shredded cheese to melt, then stirring the orzo in. The spicy, crunchy topping is the perfect final touch for a warm and comforting pan of cheesy mac—it also elevates the dish from a classic childhood comfort food to a classy meal that will be sure to impress at your next potluck or dinner party!

1. Preheat the oven to 400°F. Coat a 9 by 13-inch baking dish with nonstick cooking spray.
2. Bring a large pot of salted water to a boil over high heat. Add the orzo and cook according to package directions to al dente. Drain.
3. Bring the milk and heavy cream to a simmer in a small saucepan over low heat. While the mixture is simmering, sprinkle the cheese along the bottom of the prepared baking dish. Pour the hot milk and cream over the cheese, then add the orzo, black pepper, and salt and mix well. Top with the breadcrumbs. Bake for 25 to 30 minutes, until bubbly and golden brown on top. Serve immediately.

Serves 6 to 8

Nonstick cooking spray

1½ teaspoons kosher salt, plus more to cook the orzo

1½ pounds dried orzo

¾ cup whole milk

¾ cup heavy cream

1½ pounds sharp cheddar cheese, shredded

1½ tablespoons freshly ground black pepper

2 cups Sesame Aleppo Breadcrumbs (page 74)

To make ahead, add everything to the baking dish, breadcrumbs and all, cool completely, and refrigerate for up to 3 days before baking. Omit the Aleppo pepper from the breadcrumbs for a non-spicy version.

Edy's Tip

Herby Falafel

V, GF, NF

Would this even be a Middle Eastern cookbook without a falafel recipe? When I was growing up in Lebanon, falafel was everywhere, as an appetizer in restaurants, crushed into a sandwich, and served fresh out of the fryer by street vendors. My version is packed with herbs and lots of seeds for extra crunch. The first step of any great falafel is soaking—but not cooking—dried chickpeas until they're swollen to make the perfect mealy paste. These are equally great deep-fried or baked, or they can even go in your air fryer. Serve with plenty of tahini sauce (page 76) for drizzling.

Makes 30 falafels

1 pound dried chickpeas
   (2 cups)
1 teaspoon baking soda
4 tablespoons vegetable oil,
   plus 2 quarts if frying
½ cup chickpea flour
4 garlic cloves
1 bunch cilantro, stems
   removed (3 cups)
1 bunch parsley, stems
   removed (3 cups)
1 bunch mint, stems
   removed (3 cups)
6 scallions, roughly chopped
¼ cup fresh lemon juice
¼ cup extra-virgin olive oil
1½ tablespoons kosher salt,
   plus more as needed
1 tablespoon ground cumin
2 teaspoons Aleppo pepper
2 teaspoons baking powder
1 cup white sesame seeds
2 tablespoons nigella seeds

1. Add the chickpeas, baking soda, and 4 quarts water to a large bowl. **Soak overnight,** until the chickpeas are swollen. Drain and rinse thoroughly.

2. Preheat the oven to 450°F. Line a rimmed baking sheet with parchment paper and rub with 2 tablespoons of the vegetable oil.

3. Add the chickpeas, chickpea flour, garlic, cilantro, parsley, mint, scallions, lemon juice, olive oil, salt, cumin, Aleppo pepper, and baking powder to a food processor, working in batches as needed. Process for 3 to 4 minutes, stopping to scrape the sides as needed, until everything is fully broken down and combined into a thick green paste. Transfer the falafel mixture to a large bowl and fold in the sesame and nigella seeds.

4. Use a 3-tablespoon ice cream scoop to scoop and roll falafel balls. (Or use a tablespoon and roll three scoops together.) Arrange on the prepared baking sheet and drizzle with the remaining 2 tablespoons vegetable oil. Bake for 15 to 20 minutes, until golden brown and crisp. Season with a pinch of salt and serve immediately.

5. Alternatively, to fry, heat 2 quarts vegetable oil in a large Dutch oven over medium heat to 350°F. Fry the balls in batches for 6 to 8 minutes, until crispy and dark brown. Transfer to paper towels to drain before serving.

Edy's Tip: Baked or fried falafels can be cooled and frozen on a baking sheet until solid. Transfer to a zip-top bag and store in the freezer for up to 2 months. Reheat in the oven at 450°F for about 10 minutes, until warmed through.

Shawarma Chicken Taco Night

GF, NF

When we moved to the US, I got really into Mexican food, something we didn't have in Lebanon. (Although, fun fact, it was Lebanese immigrants in the Puebla region who first introduced Mexicans to al pastor tacos, a direct descendant of shawarma cooked on a spit.) I was especially obsessed with the taco dinner kits, which provided an easy entry to cooking for me. So taco nights became a regular event in my family, and when anyone from Lebanon came to visit it was our go-to move to impress them. When I started catering, I would do a lot of shawarma boards, which reminded me so much of my family taco nights.

Serves 6 to 8

For the marinade:

2 cups plain fat-free Greek yogurt

6 garlic cloves, grated

½ cup Shawarma Seasoning (page 22)

½ cup fresh lemon juice

¼ cup plus 4 tablespoons extra-virgin olive oil

¼ cup tomato paste

1 tablespoon kosher salt

4 pounds boneless, skinless chicken breasts, halved lengthwise

For the sides:

1 medium yellow onion, halved and thinly sliced

¼ cup chopped fresh parsley

1 tablespoon sumac

Juice of 1 lime

1 vine tomato, halved and sliced

1 head romaine or iceberg lettuce, thinly sliced

Pickle of choice (page 70), sliced

Tahini sauce of choice (page 76)

Middle Eastern Pico de Gallo (page 75)

Vermicelli Rice (page 153)

Batata Harra (page 155)

Pita, for serving

1. Make the marinade: In a large bowl, whisk together the yogurt, garlic, shawarma seasoning, lemon juice, ¼ cup of the olive oil, the tomato paste, and salt. Add the chicken and mix well to coat. Cover tightly with plastic wrap and refrigerate for at least 30 minutes or up to 24 hours.

2. Preheat the oven to 450°F. Line two rimmed baking sheets with parchment paper. Drizzle 2 tablespoons of the olive oil on each baking sheet.

3. Remove the chicken from the marinade and arrange on the prepared baking sheets. Drizzle the remaining 2 tablespoons of olive oil over each sheet of chicken. Bake for 15 to 20 minutes, until the chicken is cooked through.

4. Meanwhile, prepare the sides: In a medium bowl, toss the onion, parsley, sumac, and lime juice to combine. Set aside to marinate. Arrange the remaining sides in bowls for serving.

5. Slice the chicken and arrange it on a serving plate. Set it in the middle of the spread and let everyone stuff their own pita with chicken, onion, and the spread of toppings.

Edy's Tip: *This can be served with corn or flour tortillas for even more of a taco night vibe. Add falafel (page 164) for a flexible vegan option. This is a great Brown Paper Board for a birthday or an al fresco dinner party.*

Spatchcock Sumac Chicken

GF, NF

Chicken is my favorite protein, if you haven't noticed yet. This is a spin on a Palestinian specialty, musakhan, sumac chicken braised in vinegar until it's falling off the bone. Growing up, my grandfather Afif would grill whole chickens on the beach, and when we went to Geneva I would devour poulet roti—rotisserie chicken—like it was my job. Pulling from all those inspirations, I wanted to roast a big, sexy, showstopping chicken to really wow my guests. I love the flavors here, including the vinegar poured over while the chicken is still warm and served on the side for extra dipping.

1. Preheat the oven to 425°F.
2. Make the chicken: Pat the chicken dry and lay it breast-side down on a cutting board. Use a sharp knife or good kitchen shears to cut along either side of the spine, separating it from the ribs. Remove the spine completely and flip the chicken over, breast-side up. Push down on the breasts slightly to snap the breastbone and fully flatten the chicken. Transfer the chicken to a 12-inch cast-iron skillet.
3. Whisk the sumac, baharat, kosher salt, cumin seeds, and olive oil in a small bowl. Rub the spice mix liberally under and all over the chicken skin. Tent the chicken with aluminum foil and roast for 20 minutes. Remove the foil and roast for an additional 25 minutes, or until golden brown and the breast registers 160°F on an instant-read thermometer. (The temperature will rise while the chicken rests.) Transfer to a cutting board and let the chicken rest for 10 minutes before carving.
4. Meanwhile, make the sauce: Add the lemon juice, olive oil, and vinegar to the cast-iron skillet with any accumulated chicken juices. Set over low heat and whisk occasionally until it comes to a simmer, about 5 minutes. Remove from the heat.
5. Carve the chicken into breasts, thighs, and drumsticks. Arrange on a serving platter and spoon half of the warm sauce over the top. Transfer the rest to a small bowl to serve on the side. Garnish the chicken with the parsley and a healthy pinch of flaky sea salt before serving.

Edy's Tip: This is the moment to splurge and get a nice chicken from a local farm or butcher. The flavor will be worth the investment!

Serves 4

For the chicken:
1 (4- to 5-pound chicken)
¼ cup sumac
2 tablespoons Baharat (page 21)
2 tablespoons kosher salt
2 tablespoons cumin seeds
2 tablespoons extra-virgin olive oil

For the sauce:
½ cup fresh lemon juice
¼ cup extra-virgin olive oil
2 tablespoons apple cider vinegar
½ cup chopped fresh parsley
Flaky sea salt, for serving

Papillote Mediterranean Branzino

P, GF, NF

I learned this dish from Pamela Morgan, one of my early catering mentors. Branzino was the closest to any type of fish I would have grown up eating, and the way she prepared it so simply reminded me of home. Branzino is a flavorful, salty fish, so it doesn't need heavy sauces or lots of spices. Baking it in parchment with a few flavorful ingredients is the perfect method for drawing out the best of the fish.

Serves 6

3 tablespoons extra-virgin olive oil

2 zucchini, thinly sliced

Kosher salt and freshly ground black pepper

6 branzino fillets

½ cup sun-dried tomatoes, sliced

¼ cup pitted Kalamata olives, sliced

¼ cup drained capers

4 garlic cloves, sliced

3 sprigs fresh thyme, stems removed

1 lemon, thinly sliced, plus ½ lemon

1. Preheat the oven to 425°F. Line a rimmed baking sheet with parchment paper and rub with 1 tablespoon of the olive oil.
2. Arrange the zucchini on the prepared baking sheet and drizzle with 1 tablespoon of the remaining olive oil and a pinch of salt and pepper.
3. Lay the fillets overlapping each other on top of the zucchini. Season the fish with another pinch of salt and pepper. Sprinkle the sun-dried tomatoes, olives, capers, garlic, and thyme over the fish. Drizzle with the remaining 1 tablespoon olive oil. Shingle the lemon slices down the center of the fish. Lay another piece of parchment paper on top of the tray, tucking the corners under so the fish is completely covered. Bake for 14 minutes, rotating the tray halfway through. Peel back the parchment paper and squeeze the half lemon over the top. Serve immediately.

When I serve this at a dinner party, I love the theatrics of setting the fish on the table and lifting the parchment off for a grand reveal!

Aleppo Garlic Shrimp Cocktail

P, GF, NF

In Lebanon, we only served shrimp with the full shell on, from head to tail. So I was shocked to arrive in the US and see naked shrimp everywhere! This simple recipe uses tail-on shrimp, tossed in oil infused with the spiciness of Aleppo pepper and a bite of garlic, and finished with plenty of lemon juice. It's a simple preparation, but incredibly good. Make a big batch and serve it cold the next day as an amazing shrimp cocktail!

1. Make the oil: In a small saucepan, whisk together the garlic, Aleppo pepper, and olive oil. Set over medium-low heat, whisking occasionally, until the oil is bright red and fragrant, 10 to 12 minutes. Remove from the heat and cool for 15 minutes, then transfer to an airtight container. Refrigerate until ready to use.

2. Make the shrimp: Preheat the oven to 400°F. Line a rimmed baking sheet with parchment paper.

3. In a large bowl, toss the shrimp with the salt and ½ cup of the seasoned oil. (For extra-spicy, use ¾ cup of the oil.) Spread the shrimp evenly on the prepared baking sheet and bake for 6 to 8 minutes, until the shrimp are pink and opaque.

4. Squeeze the lemon juice over the shrimp. Serve immediately or refrigerate for at least 1 hour or overnight for a cold dish. Serve with tomato jam for dipping.

Serves 8

For the oil:

12 garlic cloves, grated

3 tablespoons Aleppo pepper

1 cup extra-virgin olive oil

For the shrimp:

2 pounds jumbo shrimp (16-20), peeled and deveined, with tails on

1 tablespoon kosher salt

Juice of ½ lemon

Spicy Tomato Jam (page 50), for serving

This makes 1 cup of seasoned oil. It can be used for frying eggs, marinating proteins, dressing salads, or drizzling over dips.

Lahm Bi Ajin Squares

This traditional Armenian dish varies wildly by region. In Beirut, it's made on crispy flatbread with lots of lemon juice. In Tripoli the lahm bi ajin is made on puff pastry and cut into squares. Growing up, once a week I would go with my grandfather Afif to Hallab 1881, a famous sweets shop in the center of Tripoli. I've always had more of a savory tooth, so I would go straight for their only savory item, the puffy squares of lahm bi ajin with a little drizzle of sweet pomegranate molasses.

Makes 24 squares

2 tablespoons unsalted butter

1 medium yellow onion, diced (1 cup)

1 pound ground beef (preferably 90% lean)

1 tablespoon kosher salt

1 tablespoon Baharat (page 21)

¼ cup pomegranate molasses

¼ cup tahini

¼ cup fresh lemon juice

1 tablespoon red wine vinegar or apple cider vinegar

2 sheets puff pastry, thawed

Pine nuts, for garnish

Lemon wedges, for serving

1. Melt the butter in a medium skillet over medium-high heat. Add the onion and sauté for 4 to 5 minutes, until translucent. Add the ground beef and use a wooden spoon to break it up. Season with the salt and baharat. Cook for 6 to 8 minutes, until the beef is no longer pink.

2. Set a colander over a bowl and drain the beef, reserving the liquid in the bowl. Set the beef in a separate medium bowl and stir in the pomegranate molasses, tahini, lemon juice, and vinegar. Taste for seasoning, then refrigerate for about 30 minutes, until cool.

3. Meanwhile, preheat the oven to 400°F. Line two rimmed baking sheets with parchment paper.

4. Lay a sheet of puff pastry on a prepared baking sheet. Cut the pastry into 12 squares by making 2 vertical cuts and 4 horizontal cuts. Separate the squares and brush with the reserved liquid from cooking the beef. Poke the squares with a fork to prevent puffing. Repeat with the remaining sheet of puff pastry on the other baking sheet. Add 1½ tablespoons of the beef mixture to the middle of each square and spread it until the square is nearly covered, leaving a ¼-inch border. Garnish with a sprinkle of pine nuts.

5. Bake for 10 minutes, then rotate the baking sheet. Bake for an additional 10 to 15 minutes, until the puff pastry is golden brown. Let cool on the baking sheet for 2 minutes, then serve warm with lemon wedges.

Pistachio-Crusted Lamb Chops

I grew up eating a lot of lamb, but it was always an event: the lamb would be slowly roasted or braised all day, resulting in a tender meat that fell right off the bone. It wasn't until college that I even knew lamb chops existed and perfecting them became a rite of passage for every culinary student. I love making these elegant chops, whether I'm serving them as a main course for a sit-down dinner or passing them as hors d'oeuvres at an event. The honey-mustard mixture adds a sweet acidity to accent the gamy lamb and the pistachio gives the chops a perfectly crunchy crust.

1. Preheat the oven to 450°F. Line a rimmed baking sheet with parchment paper.
2. Mix the kosher salt, pepper, and turmeric together in a small bowl. Rub the lamb on all sides with 2 tablespoons of the seasoning.
3. Heat the vegetable oil in a large oven-safe skillet over medium heat. When the oil is shimmering, add the lamb and sear for 7 to 9 minutes on each side, until nicely browned all over. Remove to the prepared baking sheet and let rest for 10 minutes.
4. Meanwhile, add the pistachios, panko, olive oil, and the remaining 1 tablespoon seasoning mix to a food processor. Pulse about 8 times, until smooth. In a small bowl, mix the Dijon mustard, whole grain mustard, and honey.
5. Once the lamb has rested, brush it all over with the mustard mixture, then firmly press the pistachio mixture on top. Transfer to the oven and bake for 25 to 28 minutes for medium-rare (135°F) or to your desired doneness. Remove to a cutting board and rest for 10 minutes before slicing. Finish with a sprinkle of flaky salt and serve with muhammara or tzatziki.

Serves 4

1 tablespoon kosher salt

1 tablespoon freshly ground black pepper

1 tablespoon ground turmeric

1 rack of lamb, 2 to 2½ pounds

2 tablespoons vegetable oil

¼ cup raw pistachios

½ cup panko breadcrumbs

2 tablespoons extra-virgin olive oil

1 tablespoon Dijon mustard

1 tablespoon whole grain mustard

1 tablespoon honey

Flaky sea salt, for serving

Nutty Muhammara (page 40) or Minty Tzatziki (page 39), for serving (optional)

6

Ignite Childhood Memories

The Quintessential Lebanese Staples

Edy's Tomato Sauce

V, GF, NF

Both of my grandmothers made tomato sauce all the time because it's so elemental to Lebanese cooking, as you'll see in recipes throughout the book. But it wasn't until I was working in Italy that I learned to make tomato sauce. I was put in charge of making it, and with the guidance of my sous-chef, I started working by taste to find the perfect balance. I think making tomato sauce is so seductive, letting it simmer and get darker, richer, and sexier. So take the time to enjoy the process and reap the rewards of a homemade sauce.

Makes 10 cups

1 cup extra-virgin olive oil

3 large yellow onions, diced (6 cups)

12 garlic cloves, sliced (1 cup)

1 (28-ounce) can diced tomatoes

1 (28-ounce) can crushed tomatoes

¼ cup kosher salt

¼ cup sugar

6 to 8 bay leaves

2 tablespoons dried oregano

1. Heat the olive oil in a large stockpot over medium heat. When the oil is shimmering, add the onions and sauté for 10 to 12 minutes, stirring occasionally, until translucent. Add the garlic and sauté for 3 to 4 minutes more, until soft and fragrant but not taking on any color.

2. Add the diced and crushed tomatoes to the pot, along with 2 cups water. Stir to combine, bring to a simmer, then reduce the heat to low. Stir in the salt, sugar, bay leaves, and oregano. Simmer for about 2 hours, stirring every 30 minutes to prevent scorching, until deep red and marinara consistency. Remove the bay leaves. Refrigerate in an airtight container for up to 2 weeks.

Edy's Tip: I like to double or triple the batch and freeze the extra sauce for later! Freeze in an airtight container for up to 3 months.

Chickpea & Eggplant Stew

V, GF, NF

This stew came from my catering days when I needed hearty vegan and gluten-free lunches. It is packed with protein and can be served over a variety of starches, like rice or pasta, for a satisfying and very filling winter stew. You can even add meat if you want, like Hashweh (page 74), but I don't think it needs it. It's very simply seasoned with baharat and cumin for the warm and comforting feeling of a homemade stew.

1. Make the eggplant: Preheat the oven to 400°F. Line two rimmed baking sheets with parchment paper.

2. Divide the eggplant, olive oil, salt, and cumin between the baking sheets and toss to coat. Roast for about 20 minutes, rotating the baking sheets halfway, until soft.

3. Make the stew: Add the olive oil, garlic, and cumin seeds to a large Dutch oven. Set over medium-low heat and fry for about 5 minutes, until the garlic is golden brown and crisp, taking care not to let it burn. Add the tomato sauce, bay leaves, salt, and baharat. Bring to a simmer and cook for 8 to 10 minutes, until slightly reduced. Add the chickpeas and continue simmering for about 5 minutes. Stir in the roasted eggplant and simmer for 12 to 15 minutes, until the eggplant has absorbed some of the sauce and the chickpeas are tender. Serve hot or cold with rice.

Serves 4 to 6

For the eggplant:

3 medium eggplants, partially peeled (see Tip) and cut into 2-inch cubes

6 tablespoons extra-virgin olive oil

4 teaspoons kosher salt

2 teaspoons ground cumin

For the stew:

½ cup extra-virgin olive oil

10 garlic cloves, thinly sliced (about ½ cup)

2 tablespoons cumin seeds

6 cups Edy's Tomato Sauce (page 180), or store-bought marinara

4 to 5 bay leaves

1 tablespoon kosher salt

1 tablespoon Baharat (page 21)

2 (15.5-ounce) cans chickpeas, drained and rinsed

Vermicelli Rice (page 153) or plain rice, for serving

Edy's Tip: I like to partially peel my eggplants, like a zebra. Leaving a little skin on helps hold the eggplant together so it doesn't turn into mush.

Lubiyeh Bi Zeit

V, GF

Lubiyeh bi zeit is a major dish around Lent, served hot or cold. Some people firmly insist this is mezze, but to me it's a perfect side dish or even a main meal served with rice. It reminds me of both my grandmothers: Jacquo always had a jar of it in her fridge and Odette kept a tightly wrapped bowl in hers. Every Lebanese teita had a secret stash somewhere. Mine goes easier on the olive oil than the traditional dish for a lighter (and less expensive) version.

Serves 4 to 6

5 tablespoons plus a pinch of kosher salt

2 pounds green beans, trimmed

¼ cup extra-virgin olive oil

1 tablespoon Aleppo pepper

6 cups Edy's Tomato Sauce (page 180)

3 tablespoons pomegranate molasses

1 tablespoon vegetable oil

½ cup sliced almonds

1. Bring a large pot of water to boil over high heat. Stir in 4 tablespoons of the salt, then add the green beans. Simmer for 6 to 8 minutes, until bright green and crisp-tender. Drain the beans and rinse under cold water to stop the cooking. Set aside to drain completely.

2. Meanwhile, heat the olive oil in a large saucepan over medium heat. When the oil is shimmering, add the Aleppo pepper and fry for about 1 minute, stirring constantly, until the oil is red and fragrant. Stir in the tomato sauce, pomegranate molasses, and remaining 1 tablespoon salt. Simmer for 10 to 15 minutes, until slightly reduced. Add the green beans to the sauce and simmer for 8 to 10 minutes, until the green beans are soft and the sauce is dark red.

3. While the beans are simmering, heat the vegetable oil in a small skillet over medium heat. When the oil is shimmering, add the almonds and fry until toasted, tossing occasionally, 5 to 6 minutes. Season with a pinch of salt and remove from the heat. Plate the green beans and sprinkle the almonds over the top before serving.

Nouille

This is my family's version of lasagna, the warm and gooey casserole dish that everyone gathers around. As you can likely tell, the name and techniques are heavily influenced by France's occupation of Lebanon—one of the many signs of France's lingering colonialism—and it feels very different from anything else found in our traditional food. But ultimately it has become a core part of Lebanese cooking and a comfort food classic. I take a few shortcuts to make assembly fast and easy, but the flavors and warmth are all there. I like to make it in several batches and freeze some for later, so I always have one ready to go.

Serves 4 to 6

1 pound low-moisture mozzarella cheese, shredded

8 ounces sharp white cheddar cheese, shredded

1 tablespoon kosher salt, plus more for cooking the pasta

1 tablespoon freshly ground black pepper

2 cups heavy cream

1 rotisserie chicken, cooled and shredded

1 pound frozen peas and carrots mix

1 pound egg fettuccine nests

1. Preheat the oven to 400°F.

2. In a large bowl, toss half of the mozzarella cheese, all of the cheddar cheese, and the salt and pepper together. Bring the heavy cream to a boil in a small saucepan over medium heat, then immediately pour over the cheese mixture and let sit for about 4 minutes. Stir with a wooden spoon until the cheese melts into a smooth sauce. Add the shredded chicken and frozen vegetables to the bowl. Stir to combine.

3. Bring a large pot of salted water to a boil over high heat. Add the fettuccine and cook according to the package directions for al dente. Reserve 1 cup pasta water before draining.

4. Add the pasta to the chicken mixture and toss to combine. Add the pasta water, a little at a time, to thin it out. Taste for seasoning. Transfer the mixture to a 9 by 13-inch baking dish and sprinkle the remaining half of the mozzarella cheese over the top. Bake for 25 to 30 minutes, until the cheese is melted and the sauce is bubbling. Turn the broiler to high and broil for 3 to 4 minutes, until the cheese is golden brown. Serve immediately.

To make ahead, transfer the pasta and chicken mixture to a foil pan, wrap tightly, and freeze for up to 2 months. Thaw in the refrigerator overnight and add 10 to 15 minutes to the baking time.

To Odette

It's the Saturday evening of Easter weekend and I'm sitting on the living room floor watching the Arabic version of *The Powerpuff Girls*, transfixed by the colorful visuals. My attention starts to drift from the superpowered trio of Blossom, Bubbles, and Buttercup as I hear the drawn-out sprays of my Teita (grandmother in Arabic) Odette applying her hairspray and perfume. The smell of the Cartier perfume creeps into the room, pulling my gaze away from the television right as she walks in. Carrying a small black bag, she looks at me and asks if I have money to donate to the church. Knowing the answer before I can say anything, she hands me a bill and we're off to the service.

"Al-Masīḥ qām," the congregation chants. Jesus is risen. Sitting next to Teita at the feast after church, I overhear endless disputes between her and her girlfriends, the most notable being how to properly plate riz a djej, a traditional Lebanese chicken and rice dish. It's so close in my mind, I can almost taste it: basmati rice spiced with baharat—a special seven-spice blend of allspice, black pepper, coriander, cloves, nutmeg, cinnamon, and cardamom—then cooked in homemade chicken stock and finished with a smattering of fried nuts. To refrain from cooking meat on Good Friday, Odette would always begin her prep on Thursday. She'd roast the chicken, then shred the meat and make a stock with the bones. I'd pass her house on my way home from school, smell the chicken stock, and know immediately that riz a djej was on the horizon.

Later, I'd sit in the kitchen and watch as she fried the medley of nuts in separate batches, starting with pine nuts, then pistachios, walnuts, cashews, and almonds, in that order. She laid out the nuts on a big metal tray lined with paper towels. I'd snatch a handful, and she'd yell at me, "At this rate they'll never make it to Sunday!"

At 4 a.m. on Easter Sunday, we'd walk back from the late-night feast at our church, bellies and hearts full. After a little nap, it was time to go downstairs to Odette's house and get ready for our Easter feast. She'd sauté the onions, beef, and spices, then finally add the rice, bay leaves, and chicken stock. I'd sneak away from playing games with my cousins to check on Teita and her rice. I'd sit on the countertop, mesmerized by the aromas and the pristine condition of her perfectly coiffed hair. After fluffing the rice with a fork, it was time for plating. She would load the platter with a giant pile of aromatic rice, then a layer of juicy shredded chicken, then heavy handfuls of the fried nuts. It was perfectly proportioned with the ideal amount of chicken, rice, and nuts in every spoonful.

You can smell the baharat spices wafting down Eckford Street whenever riz a djej is simmering on the stovetop at Edy's Grocer. Teita's rice has become my signature dish and the most popular item on our menu year after year. With Odette's picture hanging on top of the kitchen entrance at the Grocer, I know she is checking in on me and watching me fluff the rice before dishing out her specialty to the hungry Brooklyn crowds.

Riz a Djej

1. Rinse the rice in a fine-mesh strainer with cold water until the starch is washed off and the water runs clear. Set aside to drain.

2. Heat the butter and olive oil in a large Dutch oven over medium heat. When the butter has melted, add the onion and sauté for about 5 minutes, until translucent but not taking on any color.

3. Add the ground meat and use a wooden spoon to break it up and stir, about 10 minutes, until the meat starts to brown. Stir the rice, salt, and baharat into the pot and toast the rice for about 2 minutes, stirring often, until coated in the spices. Add the chicken stock, ¼ cup water, the shredded chicken, and the bay leaves. Bring to a simmer, then cover, reduce the heat to low, and simmer for 20 to 25 minutes, until the rice is cooked. Remove from the heat and use a fork to fluff the rice.

4. Pile the rice on a serving platter. Cover with the fried nut mix and pomegranate seeds and serve with plenty of yogurt on the side.

Serves 4 to 6

2 cups basmati rice

2 tablespoons unsalted butter

1 tablespoon extra-virgin olive oil

1 small yellow onion, diced (about 1 cup)

1 pound ground beef (preferably 90% lean) or ground lamb

2 tablespoons kosher salt

3 tablespoons Baharat (page 21)

4 cups low-sodium chicken stock

1 rotisserie chicken, shredded

5 to 6 bay leaves

2 cups Fried Nut Mix (page 81), for serving

2 tablespoons pomegranate seeds, for serving

Plain Greek yogurt, for serving

Samkeh Harra

P, GF

My paternal grandmother, Odette, made an incredible samkeh harra, meaning spicy fish, and everyone in Anfeh knew it. Her method was labor intensive—cooking the fish, flaking it, and baking it in a casserole with tahini sauce. I've adapted it into an easier deconstructed version, with a whole roasted fish and tahini sauce made separately. I like branzino, but red snapper, sea bass, or any mild, flaky white fish works great. It was one of her signature dishes that she never got the chance to teach me. I wish we had more time so I could have learned.

Serves 4 to 6

For the fish:

2 whole branzino or 6 branzino fillets, about 2 pounds total

Kosher salt

Extra-virgin olive oil

1 lemon, thinly sliced

2 tablespoons toasted pine nuts or Fried Nut Mix (page 81), for serving

Chopped fresh parsley, for serving

For the sauce:

2 tablespoons extra-virgin olive oil

1 small yellow onion, diced (about 1 cup)

3 scallions, thinly sliced (about ½ cup)

4 garlic cloves, grated

2 tablespoons harissa paste

1 teaspoon Aleppo pepper

2 teaspoons kosher salt

1 bunch fresh cilantro, including stems, chopped (about 2 cups)

1 cup tahini

¾ cup fresh lemon juice

1. Make the fish: Preheat the oven to 400°F. Line a rimmed baking sheet with parchment paper.

2. Pat the fish all over with paper towels to thoroughly dry. Season with a few large pinches of salt to coat the inside flesh and outer skin. Drizzle inside and out with olive oil and use clean hands to rub it all in. Stuff with the lemon slices. Arrange the fish on the prepared baking sheet and roast in the oven for 18 to 20 minutes, until the flesh is opaque. (For fillets, roast for 8 to 10 minutes.)

3. Make the sauce: Heat the olive oil in a small saucepan over medium heat. When the oil is shimmering, add the onion and sauté for about 5 minutes, until translucent but not taking on any color. Stir in the scallions and garlic and sauté until softened, about 3 minutes. Add the harissa paste, Aleppo pepper, and 1 teaspoon of the salt. Stir until the harissa paste is a deep red and completely mixed into the aromatics. Add the cilantro and ¼ cup water to thin the sauce. Stir until the cilantro is wilted. Turn the heat off and remove the mixture to a small bowl.

4. In the same saucepan, add the tahini, lemon juice, remaining 1 teaspoon salt, and 1 cup cold water. Whisk together until completely combined. Set over low heat and let the tahini sauce slowly simmer for about 10 minutes, stirring, until thickened. This is an emulsion, so the constant motion keeps the fat from separating and the tahini from scorching. Once the sauce thickens, whisk in the onion mixture.

5. When the fish is ready, take it out of the oven and rest it on the baking sheet for 4 minutes. Transfer to a serving platter, spoon the sauce over the top, and garnish with the nuts and parsley. Serve immediately.

Kibbeh Three Ways

Kibbeh is the Middle East's answer to meatloaf. Instead of breadcrumbs, we use bulgur to bind everything together, and it's spiced with the warm flavors of baharat. It can be formed into patties or balls or layered up. As any Middle Eastern immigrant will tell you, kibbeh is the most nostalgic reminder of childhood.

Serves 4 to 6

The Mother Base

1. Soak the bulgur in a large bowl with 3 cups warm water for 30 minutes. Drain and set aside.
2. Grate the onions using a box grater or by roughly chopping then pulsing about 6 times in a food processor until a paste forms. Transfer the onion paste to a fine-mesh strainer and use a spoon to press and extract all the liquid. Discard the liquid. Add the strained onions to a large bowl.
3. Press the bulgur to squeeze out any excess water. Add the bulgur, baharat, and salt to the onions and mix well. Add the ground beef and mix until combined. From here, the kibbeh is ready to be formed into any of the following dishes.

1½ cups fine bulgur

2 medium yellow onions

3 tablespoons Baharat (page 21)

2 tablespoons kosher salt

1 pound ground beef (preferably 90% lean)

One Layer

1. Preheat the oven to 450°F. Lightly coat two rimmed baking sheets with the olive oil.
2. Scoop and roll the kibbeh mixture into balls, about ¼ cup each, and dip your hands in ice water to prevent sticking, then press into a patty. Arrange the patties across the surface of the baking sheets, pressing into an even layer that covers each sheet. Use a paring knife to cut 4 lines in one direction, then rotate the pan and cut 5 lines to make squares. Use the knife and a fork to create designs in each square. (For example, use the end of the fork to press diagonal lines, use the tines to poke holes, etc.) Once the kibbeh is decorated, drizzle the vegetable oil evenly over both sheets and use your hands to spread it over the entire surface. Bake for 20 to 25 minutes, until the surface is crisp. Cool on the baking sheets for about 8 minutes, then slice and serve with a side of Greek yogurt or minty tzatziki.

¼ cup extra-virgin olive oil

The Mother Base (see above)

½ cup vegetable oil

Plain Greek yogurt or Minty Tzatziki (page 39), for serving

(cont.)

Three Layer

2 tablespoons extra-virgin olive oil

Double batch of the Mother Base (page 191)

2 cups Hashweh (page 74)

¼ cup vegetable oil

Plain Greek yogurt or Minty Tzatziki (page 39), for serving

1. Preheat the oven to 450°F. Rub a 9 by 13-inch baking dish with the olive oil.

2. Divide the kibbeh base in half. Scoop and roll half of the kibbeh mixture into balls, about ¼ cup each, dipping your hands in ice water to prevent sticking, then press into a patty. Arrange the patties across the surface of the baking sheets, pressing into an even layer that covers the dish. Spread the hashweh evenly over the bottom layer, then scoop and press the remaining kibbeh evenly over the top. Use wet hands to smooth the surface of the kibbeh.

3. Use a paring knife to cut the top layer down the center vertically, then rotate the baking dish and cut the top layer four times horizontally to make squares. Use the knife and a fork to create designs in each square. (For example, dashes, holes, etc.) Poke a hole in the center all the way to the bottom of the dish to aid in even cooking. Once the kibbeh is decorated, drizzle the vegetable oil evenly over both sheets and use your hands to spread it over the entire surface. Bake for 40 to 45 minutes, until the surface is crisp. Cool in the baking dish for about 8 minutes, then slice and serve with a side of Greek yogurt or minty tzatziki.

Balls

The Mother Base (page 191)

2 cups Hashweh (page 74)

¼ cup extra-virgin olive oil

Plain Greek yogurt or Minty Tzatziki (page 39), for serving

1. Preheat the oven to 450°F. Line a rimmed baking sheet with parchment paper.

2. Scoop the kibbeh into ¼-cup portions, roll into balls, and arrange on the prepared baking sheet. Press a cavity in the center of each ball and fill with 2 to 3 teaspoons hashweh. Re-form the kibbeh into an oval ball around the hashweh like a football.

3. Drizzle the balls with the olive oil and bake for about 15 minutes, until browned and cooked through. Rest on the baking sheet for 5 minutes, then arrange on a serving platter with a side of Greek yogurt or minty tzatziki.

4. Alternatively, to fry, heat 2 quarts of vegetable oil in a large Dutch oven over medium heat to 350°F. Fry the balls in batches for 6 to 8 minutes, until crispy and dark brown. Transfer to paper towels to drain before serving.

To Jacqueline

Jacquo, my maternal grandmother, was the queen of kibbeh. She only made it in large batches, usually fifteen pounds of ground meat at a time, turning out baked layered pans, rolled balls, round patties, and (my favorite) a raw tartare known as kibbeh nayyeh.

For kibbeh nayyeh, the meat had to be preordered from the best butcher in town and picked up that morning, so it was fresh, fresh, fresh. She handled it with such delicacy. She skipped the bulgur but added lots of red pepper paste. The onions had to be finely pulsed and squeezed to make sure no extra water diluted the mixture. She used ice water to keep her hands cold while mixing and shaping the kibbeh.

When it came to cooked kibbeh, she worked quickly and efficiently. I always admired her hands as she formed the kibbeh balls, rolling them tight then slowly piercing the center and twisting to make the hole deep enough for a spoonful of hashweh, a spiced meat mixture. Her layered kibbeh pans were a master class in decoration. She would use a fork, knife, and spoon to make beautiful, surprisingly intricate designs. I loved when she would summon my sister and me into the kitchen and give us each a fork to decorate a square or two in the pan. After rolling all her balls, shaping all her patties, and building all her pans, she would load up the freezer in case someone dropped by unannounced, in the event of a family emergency, or for the moments when you told her you weren't hungry but she decided you needed something to eat anyway.

That was her way, the freezing way. My grandparents lived in Beirut, but my grandfather Edouard worked in Aleppo, so Jacquo traveled and hosted a lot between the two cities and had to think ahead when it came to dinner parties—batching, wrapping, and freezing for the next occasion. She was militant about her freezer organization and knew exactly what she had in stock at all times—usually a mix of stuffed hand pies, homemade Aleppo mortadella, chicken escalope, filled grape leaves, gratin casseroles, hashweh-stuffed zucchini, and, of course, containers of tomato sauce, chicken stock, and a variety of nuts and spices to keep them as fresh as possible.

On New Year's Day, Jacquo always threw the most beautiful lunch. Everything was white, from the tablecloth to the plates. Her centerpiece was kibbeh bi laban, kibbeh balls in a pool of yogurt sauce (in keeping with the white theme). For this special occasion, she didn't just dig up some kibbeh balls from the freezer. She made a special batch, stuffed with hashweh. One special kibbeh got an olive in the center and whoever found that one would have good luck in the new year. The rest of the kibbeh balls were stuffed with a little Aleppo pepper oil, so when they burst the red oil would swirl around in the minty yogurt sauce. The most difficult part was not staining my shirt while spooning the beautifully cooked yogurt sauce and carefully stuffed kibbeh balls with plenty of pine nuts to go around.

Jacquo's freezing habits have stuck with me to this day, and in fact I wouldn't be able to be the multitasker I am today without her guidance. Between the Grocer and catering orders, I am always planning ahead and trying to stay on top of my to-do lists. Preparing dishes in big batches has become my standard, from mezze to meats to stocks. Learning how to freeze, and maintaining an organized freezer, is a skill I am proud to have because not only does it save time, it also saves food, waste, and money. Even though no one can make kibbeh like Jacquo used to make, I still keep her Syrian influence in my everyday cooking. All these little habits and tricks that I learned from the ladies of my childhood are things I keep alive today in my Brooklyn kitchen to make our work seamless and fun!

Kibbeh Bi Laban

Serves 4 to 6

2 (32-ounce) containers plain fat-free Greek yogurt

½ cup fresh lemon juice (from 2 to 3 lemons)

3 tablespoons kosher salt

1 tablespoon cornstarch

1 tablespoon dried mint, plus more for garnish

Kibbeh Balls (page 192)

Pine nuts or Aleppo Chili Crisp (page 78), for garnish

1. In a large pot, stir together the yogurt, lemon juice, salt, and 1½ cups water. In a small bowl, whisk the cornstarch and ½ cup water to form a smooth slurry, then stir it into the pot. Set over medium-low heat. Cook, stirring constantly so the yogurt doesn't scorch, until the mixture starts to thicken like a bechamel, 15 to 18 minutes. Stir in the dried mint and taste for seasoning.

2. Add the kibbeh balls to the yogurt. If they're cold, simmer for 8 to 10 minutes to warm through. If they're fresh, simmer for 2 minutes to marry the flavors. Garnish with more dried mint and pine nuts or a drizzle of oil from the chili crisp.

Fatteh Six Ways

Centuries before New Yorkers were lining up for healthy bowl lunches, the Middle East was making fatteh, a sort of loosely assembled meal of veggies, balila, yogurt, and tahini topped with crispy pita pieces. For catering orders, I make mine vegan and gluten-free without the yogurt and pita and use nuts for crunch instead, but feel free to customize however you want—anything can go in the bowl. In the summer of 2022, in Lebanon, I had my first shrimp fatteh, and it blew me away. So I was inspired to branch out from the produce aisle and include two protein options as well. If you're feeling ambitious, you can prep a few options and set them out for friends at your next casual dinner party!

Serves 4 to 6

Rainbow Carrot
V, GF

1. Preheat the oven to 400°F. Line a rimmed baking sheet with parchment paper.
2. Add the carrots to the baking sheet. Drizzle with the olive oil and sprinkle with the salt, cumin seeds, and sugar. Toss to coat. Roast for about 30 minutes, until the carrots are browned and tender.
3. Arrange the carrots in a serving bowl or rimmed platter. Spoon the balila and tahini dressing over the top, then garnish with the pine nuts before serving.

8 to 10 (2 pounds) large rainbow carrots, cut into 1-inch pieces

2 tablespoons extra-virgin olive oil

1 tablespoon kosher salt

1 tablespoon cumin seeds

2 teaspoons sugar

1½ cups Balila (page 66)

1 cup Cilantro Lime Tahini (page 76)

2 tablespoons toasted pine nuts

(cont.)

Cauliflower

V, GF

1 large head (2 to 3 pounds) cauliflower, broken into florets

3 tablespoons extra-virgin olive oil

2 tablespoons Za'atar (page 23) or store-bought za'atar

2 teaspoons kosher salt

1½ cups Balila (page 66)

1 cup Sweet Tahini or Caesar Tahini (page 76)

¼ cup chopped walnuts, toasted

1. Preheat the oven to 400°F. Line a rimmed baking sheet with parchment paper.
2. Add the cauliflower to the baking sheet. Drizzle with the olive oil and sprinkle with the za'atar and salt. Toss to coat. Roast for about 25 minutes, until the cauliflower is fork-tender.
3. Arrange the cauliflower in a serving bowl or rimmed platter. Spoon the balila and tahini dressing over the top, then garnish with the walnuts before serving.

Eggplant & Zucchini

V, GF

2 medium (1 pound) zucchini, cut into 1-inch pieces

1 large (1 pound) eggplant, partially peeled and cut into 1-inch pieces

3 tablespoons extra-virgin olive oil

2 tablespoons sumac

2 tablespoons sesame seeds

1 tablespoon kosher salt

1½ cups Balila (page 66)

1 cup Spicy Tahini (page 76)

¼ cup chopped raw pistachios

1. Preheat the oven to 400°F. Line a rimmed baking sheet with parchment paper.
2. Add the zucchini and eggplant to the baking sheet. Drizzle with the olive oil and sprinkle with the sumac, sesame seeds, and salt. Toss to coat. Roast for 20 to 25 minutes, until the vegetables are browned and tender.
3. Arrange the vegetables in a serving bowl or rimmed platter. Spoon the balila and tahini dressing over the top, then garnish with the pistachios before serving.

Fall Squash

V, GF

1. Preheat the oven to 400°F. Line a rimmed baking sheet with parchment paper.
2. Add the delicata and butternut squash to the baking sheet. Drizzle with the olive oil and maple syrup and sprinkle with the salt and Aleppo pepper. Toss to coat. Roast for 35 to 40 minutes, until the squash is slightly caramelized and tender.
3. Arrange the squash in a serving bowl or rimmed platter. Spoon the balila and tahini dressing over the top, then garnish with the cashews before serving.

1 pound delicata squash, halved, seeded, and cut into 1-inch-thick half moons

1 (1- to 2-pound) pound butternut squash, peeled, halved, seeded, and cut into 2-inch pieces

3 tablespoons extra-virgin olive oil

3 tablespoons pure maple syrup

1 tablespoon kosher salt

1 tablespoon Aleppo pepper

½ batch Balila (page 66)

1 cup Cilantro Lime Tahini (page 76)

¼ cup chopped cashews, toasted

(cont.)

If you're looking for a little more oomph in your fatteh bowl, go ahead and add 1 cup Greek yogurt to the tahini sauce and crumble pita chips on top.

Edy's Tip

Shawarma Chicken

GF

1 rotisserie chicken, shredded

2 cups low-sodium chicken stock or water

4 tablespoons Shawarma Seasoning (page 22) or store-bought shawarma seasoning

1 teaspoon kosher salt

½ batch Balila (page 66)

1 cup any tahini sauce (page 76)

¼ cup toasted pepitas or Fried Nut Mix (page 81)

1. Add the shredded chicken, chicken stock, shawarma seasoning, and salt to a medium saucepan over medium heat. Bring to a simmer and cook for 4 to 5 minutes, until the chicken is warmed through and seasoned. Remove from the heat and let cool for 5 minutes, then taste for seasoning.

2. Arrange the chicken and stock in a serving bowl or rimmed platter. Spoon the balila and tahini dressing over the top, then garnish with the pepitas before serving.

Shrimp

P, GF, NF

2 pounds shrimp, peeled, tails off, and deveined

2 tablespoons extra-virgin olive oil

3 tablespoons Edy's Everything Seasoning (page 23) or store-bought everything bagel seasoning

½ batch Balila (page 66)

1 cup Basil Lemon Tahini (page 76)

Crumbled tortilla chips, for garnish

1. Preheat the oven to 400°F. Line a rimmed baking sheet with parchment paper.

2. Add the shrimp to the baking sheet. Drizzle with the olive oil and sprinkle with the everything seasoning. Toss to coat. Roast for 6 to 8 minutes, until the shrimp are cooked through.

3. Arrange the shrimp in a serving bowl or rimmed platter. Spoon the balila and tahini dressing over the top, then garnish with the tortilla chips before serving.

7

Helou ya Helou

Salty Chocolate Tahini Cookie

VG, NF

Everyone needs a signature chocolate chip cookie—it's just the rule of working in the American food scene. I had so much fun developing this one because I think it really speaks to who I am. I love salt on my dessert (I was born with more of a savory tooth), and the tahini adds a silky richness that helps balance the cookie, which is sweetened with a mixture of sugar and date molasses. Big chunks of chocolate get mixed into the batter—made with regular and chickpea flour, for extra density and flavor—along with sesame seeds that get crunchy and nutty as they bake. It's my idea of cookie perfection!

Makes 20 cookies

1½ cups all-purpose flour

1½ cups chickpea flour

1 teaspoon baking powder

1 cup (2 sticks) unsalted butter, at room temperature

1 packed cup light brown sugar

¼ cup granulated sugar

¼ cup date molasses

¼ cup tahini

2 large eggs, at room temperature

1 tablespoon kosher salt

8 ounces 70% bittersweet chocolate, chopped

3 tablespoons sesame seeds

2 teaspoons flaky sea salt

1. In a medium bowl, sift together the all-purpose flour, chickpea flour, and baking powder.

2. In a stand mixer fitted with the paddle attachment, or in a large bowl with an electric hand mixer, beat the butter, brown sugar, granulated sugar, date molasses, and tahini on medium speed until fully combined and fluffy, about 3 minutes, stopping to scrape down the sides as needed. Beat in the eggs, one at a time, and the kosher salt, until combined, about 2 minutes, stopping to scrape down the sides before adding the flour. Reduce the speed to low and add the flour mixture in three parts. Mix until just combined, being careful not to overwork. Remove the bowl from the stand mixer. Add the chocolate and sesame seeds and fold to combine.

3. Line a rimmed baking sheet with parchment paper. Use a large cookie scoop, or measure 3 tablespoons, to roll the dough into balls and arrange on the baking sheet. Refrigerate for 1 hour or overnight.

4. Preheat the oven to 350°F.

5. Remove the baking sheet from the refrigerator and sprinkle the dough balls with flaky sea salt. Bake for 10 to 12 minutes, until the cookies have spread and the edges are golden brown. Let cool on the baking sheet for 5 minutes, then transfer to a wire rack to finish cooling. Store in an airtight container at room temperature for up to 5 days.

Edy's Tip: *Scoop the dough into balls and freeze on a baking sheet until solid. Transfer to a zip-top bag and store in the freezer to bake whenever you want one or a whole batch.*

Pistachio Halva Rice Krispy

These are a bestseller at the Grocer around the holidays. It's mostly a classic Rice Krispie, except that crushed pistachio halva gets mixed in, adding surprise bursts of flavor. For those who don't know, halva is a sweetened tahini (sesame paste) that's cooked until it's hard and crumbly. It's incredible. The final touch is a pool of chocolate on top with a sprinkle of chopped pistachios for a little crunch and a bright green accent. We only make them once a year, but they're perfect all the time!

Makes 20 bars

1. Melt the butter in a medium saucepan over medium heat. Once the butter is fully melted, add the marshmallows and salt and stir until the marshmallows are melted and incorporated into the butter.
2. In a large bowl, add the cereal and pour the marshmallow mixture over the top. Stir to combine, then crumble in the halva and mix again. Transfer the mixture to a rimmed baking sheet and use wet hands to press and spread evenly across the entire sheet. Refrigerate for about 1 hour, until it's firm.
3. Pour the chocolate chips into a medium heatproof bowl. Heat the heavy cream in a small saucepan over medium heat until it just starts to simmer. Pour the hot cream over the chocolate chips and let sit for 5 minutes. Whisk until a smooth, glossy sauce forms, then drizzle on top of the chilled bars. Sprinkle the pistachios on top, then cut into 20 bars before serving. Store, covered, at room temperature for up to 3 days.

10 tablespoons unsalted butter

12 cups mini marshmallows

1 tablespoon kosher salt

4 quarts Rice Krispies or other crisped rice cereal

10 ounces pistachio halva

1 (12-ounce) bag dark chocolate chips

1 cup heavy cream

¼ cup pistachios, chopped

For a finer pistachio garnish, grate the nuts on a rasp grater over the bars to make a vibrant green dust.

To Oprah

Anfeh has always been a tight-knit village. Everyone knows each other and everyone is somehow your second cousin once removed. It was also a deeply religious place, proudly Greek Orthodox with one of the oldest churches in the world, Saydet el Rih. Church was the center of the community, a place to worship and come together. A strong religious presence also meant being gay was something that went unspoken.

Growing up in the early nineties, I spent a lot of time at Institut Paola, my mom's beauty salon. I didn't realize it at the time, but I was surrounded by gay men. I couldn't pinpoint why they seemed different from my dad's friends. As a child I was always running around doing the most (shocking, I know!), and it didn't go unnoticed by my family. My mom would tell me to straighten my wrist, or my grandmother would say "tighten your jaw," meaning "you sound feminine." My dad would ask me why I was dancing to Nancy Ajram music videos instead of playing video games, or my grandpa would wonder aloud why I was playing with my sister and her girlfriends instead of the boys.

When we moved to America, things got even worse. I felt so alone—not only was I not like the other boys, I was a complete outsider. I couldn't speak English, so I couldn't stick up for myself during recess. My dad signed me up for football and I somehow played for seven years, taking the tackling, slurs, and gay jokes season after season.

I kept suppressing these feelings and turned to food (and Oprah) for comfort. I would race home from school just in time to catch *The Oprah Winfrey Show* at 4 p.m. With a bowl of Cheez-Its and a can of Diet Coke in hand, I would watch, learn, cry, and grow. The way she carried herself reminded me of all the strong women in my life and brought me hope, joy, confidence, and a sprinkle of positivity. Her interviews with people from all sorts of paths opened my eyes to another world of humanity. From 2004 until 2011, Oprah guided me through tough times and helped me build confidence, sixty minutes at a time.

The Oprah Winfrey Show ended during my junior year of high school, on the same day that I got my driver's license. It was an emotional goodbye for me, but when the show ended I felt like I had graduated from her academy and was ready to live my life on my own terms. When my senior year of high school began, I started sticking up for myself and finding my voice, purpose, values, and confidence. It put me on the path to culinary school and pursuing my passion for cooking. My junior year of college, I built enough confidence to come out to one of my friends. This simple act was the beginning of everything—the first step toward shedding the repressed feelings, religious oppression, bullying, and internalized hate toward the idea of being gay.

Oprah would always say, "Surround yourself with only people who are going to lift you higher," and when I left college and moved to New York, that's what I started to do. I started building my chosen family and finding my voice through food. Whenever I was invited somewhere, I would always bring a log of biscuit au chocolat, and it started to become part of my identity. *Biscuit au chocolat*, also known as "chocolate biscuit" or "chocolate salami" as the Italians say, is a cookie I grew up with in Lebanon and cherished. It was an easy recipe that was more than the sum of its parts. Fudgy, crunchy, and salty, it was perfect for any occasion. The waves of compliments brought me so much joy and helped me find my confidence—both inside and outside the kitchen.

The biscuit au chocolat ended up becoming the push I needed to start my catering business. One prep day after another, I found myself back in the kitchen pouring hot cream on top of dark chocolate morsels, swirling the mixture as it melted, cracking the tea cookies into the chocolate pool, and rolling them into fat logs. Batch after batch, my catering business grew as I stepped into my culture, my confidence, and myself. I found the strength to come out to my parents and finally face my fear of identifying as a "Gay Lebanese Chef."

I am so proud of that little boy from Anfeh, the one who loves the beach, his morning manoushe, and *The Oprah Winfrey Show*. Without his hopes, dreams, wishes, ambition, and confidence, Edy's Grocer and my lemony corner in Brooklyn would have never existed. And to Oprah, I hope one day I will be able to reciprocate everything you have done for me. Thank you for being my guardian and greatest teacher.

Biscuit au Chocolat

VG, NF

Makes 45 cookies

2 (12-ounce) bags
    semisweet chocolate
    chips
1 tablespoon kosher salt
2 cups heavy cream
3 (7-ounce) packages
    Marie biscuits or 1½
    (14.4-ounce) boxes
    graham crackers
Flaky sea salt, for serving

1. Pour the chocolate chips and kosher salt into a medium heatproof bowl. Heat the heavy cream in a small saucepan over medium heat until it just starts to simmer. Pour the hot cream over the chocolate chips and let sit for 5 minutes. Whisk until a smooth, glossy sauce forms. Crumble the cookies into the ganache, in uneven 1- to 2-inch pieces. Fold to combine.

2. Lay a 12-inch piece of parchment paper on a work surface. Scrape a third of the cookie mixture into the center of the parchment. Fold the parchment over itself and form the cookie mixture into a log about 3 inches in diameter. Wrap tightly with the parchment, then wrap in foil. Repeat two more times with the remaining cookie mixture. Freeze the logs for at least 4 hours or overnight, until completely firm.

3. When ready to serve, unwrap the desired number of logs and cut into 1-inch-thick rounds. Garnish with flaky sea salt and serve immediately. Store in the freezer for up to 2 months.

Edy's Tip

These cookies are no-bake, perfect for when you want something sweet but it's too hot for the oven. Even better: The logs keep in the freezer for up to 2 months. I like to always keep a batch handy for an immediate dessert!

Salted Tahini Brownie

VG, NF

Growing up, I made a lot of boxed brownies. I would bring them to school events or friends' houses and always had fun adding in new ingredients. To this day, I believe that a boxed brownie is the best brownie. I'm not afraid to admit it, and I'm ready to die on that hill. I do make a few small adjustments to improve an already perfect dessert. I add Greek yogurt (I mean, when *don't* I add Greek yogurt?), which makes everything unbelievably soft and moist, and extra chocolate chips because why not! A rich tahini swirl, a scattering of sesame seeds, and a big pinch of flaky salt finish off the job and no one needs to know your shortcut! Cut them into mini squares to serve a group or big pieces for the base of a sundae.

1. Preheat the oven to 350°F. Coat an 8 by 8-inch baking dish with nonstick spray.

2. In a medium bowl, whisk together the egg, yogurt, and kosher salt. Add ⅓ cup water plus the vegetable oil, brownie mix, and chocolate chips. Whisk until fully incorporated, scraping down the bowl as needed.

3. Pour the batter into the prepared baking dish. Drizzle the tahini over the batter, then use a skewer or butter knife to swirl the tahini into the batter. Sprinkle the sesame seeds and flaky sea salt over the top. Bake for 30 to 35 minutes, until a toothpick inserted in the center comes out clean. Let the brownie cool in the baking dish for 10 minutes, then cut into 12 bars. Serve them hot out of the oven with labneh mousse or ice cream or refrigerate for up to 1 week and let come to room temperature before serving.

Makes 12 brownies

Nonstick cooking spray
1 large egg
⅓ cup plain fat-free Greek yogurt
1 tablespoon kosher salt
⅓ cup vegetable oil
1 box brownie mix, preferably Ghirardelli
¼ cup bittersweet chocolate chips
2 tablespoons tahini
1 teaspoon sesame seeds
½ teaspoon flaky sea salt
Labneh Mousse (page 215) or ice cream, for serving

Spicy Chocolate Popcorn

V, GF, NF

During the early pandemic days, I ordered a popcorn machine for my nightly Netflix. (I was a lethal mix of bored and anxious and needed something to keep my mind occupied.) I started playing around to dress up my popcorn, adding herbs, spices, and sauces, and this one stuck as my favorite. The two rules are you have to eat it right away and it makes a total mess, so put a bib on you and a tablecloth on the couch to be safe. It's a rare dessert that's vegan, gluten-free, nut-free, and not lacking in any indulgence.

Serves 4

1 cup bittersweet
  chocolate chips
½ cup tahini
1 tablespoon Aleppo
  pepper
½ cup oat milk
¼ cup vegetable oil
1 cup popcorn kernels
1 teaspoon kosher salt
2 tablespoons sesame
  seeds
1 tablespoon flaky sea
  salt

1. Add the chocolate chips, tahini, and Aleppo pepper to a medium heatproof bowl. Heat the oat milk in a small saucepan over medium heat until it just starts to simmer. Pour the hot milk over the chocolate chips and let sit for 5 minutes. Whisk until a smooth, glossy sauce forms.

2. Heat the vegetable oil in a large saucepan over medium heat. When the oil is shimmering, add the popcorn kernels and kosher salt. Swirl the saucepan to coat the kernels in oil, then cover and reduce the heat to low. Shake the saucepan occasionally as the kernels start popping. When the popping has slowed to a pop every couple seconds, remove from the heat and pour the popcorn into a large bowl.

3. Drizzle the chocolate sauce over the popcorn and mix to coat. Top with the sesame seeds and flaky sea salt before serving.

Labneh Mousse

This recipe originally started as an ice cream, part of a pop-up dinner, and my friend and fellow chef Eric See helped me develop it. For making it at home, I adapted it into something between an ice cream and mousse, because it's easier and less fussy, and played around with flavors to produce three very unexpected (and delicious!) treats. Eating this always brings me back to summer nights in Italy, enjoying rich and creamy desserts like panna cotta or affogato. I recommend setting it in a big bowl and letting everyone scoop out their own serving.

Makes 1½ quarts

Rose & Pistachio
VG, GF

1. In a stand mixer fitted with the whisk attachment, beat the heavy cream and powdered sugar to stiff peaks. (Alternatively, use a large bowl and an electric hand mixer.)
2. In a large bowl, use a rubber spatula to swirl and spread the labneh and rosewater until it's nice and loose. Add one-third of the whipped cream and fold it in. Add the remaining whipped cream in two parts, folding to combine. Finally, fold in the pistachios. Cover and refrigerate for at least 1 hour or overnight.

2 cups heavy cream
¾ cup powdered sugar
1 pound store-bought full-fat labneh, at room temperature
3 tablespoons rosewater
½ cup chopped pistachios

Olive Oil & Chocolate
VG, GF, NF

1. In a stand mixer fitted with the whisk attachment, beat the heavy cream and powdered sugar to stiff peaks. (Alternatively, use a large bowl and an electric hand mixer.)
2. In a large bowl, use a rubber spatula to swirl and spread the labneh and olive oil until it's nice and loose. Add one-third of the whipped cream and fold it in. Add the remaining whipped cream in two parts, folding to combine. Finally, fold in the chocolate and salt. Cover and refrigerate for at least 1 hour or overnight.

2 cups heavy cream
¾ cup powdered sugar
1 pound store-bought full-fat labneh, at room temperature
¼ cup extra-virgin olive oil
2 ounces bittersweet chocolate, chopped
1 teaspoon kosher salt

(cont.)

Lemon, Fennel & Pine Nut

VG, GF

2 cups heavy cream

¾ cup powdered sugar

1 pound store-bought
full-fat labneh, at
room temperature

Zest of 1 lemon

¼ cup fresh lemon juice

3 tablespoons pine nuts

1 teaspoon toasted
fennel seeds

1. In a stand mixer fitted with the whisk attachment, beat the heavy cream and powdered sugar to stiff peaks. (Alternatively, use a large bowl and an electric hand mixer.)

2. In a large bowl, use a rubber spatula to swirl and spread the labneh with the lemon zest and juice until it's nice and loose. Add one-third of the whipped cream and fold it in. Add the remaining whipped cream in two parts, folding to combine. Finally, fold in the pine nuts and fennel seeds. Cover and refrigerate for at least 1 hour or overnight.

Orange Blossom Osmalieh

VG

The Queen of the Desserts. I first made this after a client requested it for a catering event.
I was scared out of my mind and bought triple the amount of ingredients so I would have
plenty of room for error. It turns out it wasn't too hard at all, and I found I could tackle
each element separately ahead of time and assemble just before serving, which makes
it absolutely perfect for any event or dinner party. Shredded phyllo gets baked like cake
layers, a rosewater cream filling gets sandwiched between them, and orange blossom syrup
saturates all the layers. It's rich, fragrant, and a total showstopper.

Serves 8

For the base:
Nonstick cooking spray
2 (1-pound) boxes
    frozen shredded
    phyllo dough, thawed
2 cups (4 sticks)
    unsalted butter,
    melted
Chopped pistachios
    and crushed rose
    petals, for garnish

For the filling:
1 cup heavy cream
¼ cup confectioners'
    sugar
3 tablespoons
    rosewater
2 cups mascarpone
    cheese, at room
    temperature
¼ cup finely crumbled
    feta cheese

For the syrup:
1 cup granulated sugar
¼ cup orange blossom
    water

1. Make the base: Preheat the oven to 400°F. Coat two 9-inch cake
pans with nonstick spray.
2. In a medium bowl, toss the shredded phyllo with the melted
butter until fully coated. Divide in half and press into the bottom of
each prepared cake pan until flat and compacted. Bake for 25 to 30
minutes, rotating the pans halfway, until the pastry is crisp and golden
brown. Cool in the pans for about 20 minutes, until the pastry is set,
then turn out onto a wire rack or paper towel to drain the excess fat.
(This step can be done up to 1 day ahead, covered and stored at room
temperature, and filled when ready to serve.)
3. Make the filling: Add the heavy cream, confectioners' sugar, and
rosewater to a large bowl. Use an electric hand mixer to whip the cream
to soft peaks. In a separate medium bowl, fold the mascarpone and
feta cheeses together until soft and spreadable. Add one-third of the
whipped cream to the mascarpone and fold until incorporated. Add the
remaining cream in two parts, folding each in to incorporate. Transfer
the mixture to a piping bag fitted with a star tip (or a large zip-top bag)
and refrigerate until ready to assemble. (This step can be done and
refrigerated up to 1 day ahead.)
4. Make the syrup: In a small saucepan, add 1 cup water with the sugar
and orange blossom water. Set over medium heat, bring to a simmer,
and cook for 15 minutes without stirring, until the sugar has dissolved
and the mixture is a little syrupy. Let it cool. (This step can be done up
to 1 day ahead. Transfer to a jar and refrigerate.)
5. To assemble, set one disc of baked phyllo dough on a cake stand or
serving plate. Brush with ¼ cup of the orange blossom syrup. Pipe the
mascarpone cream in a circular motion to fully cover the phyllo. (Snip
the corner off the zip-top bag, if using.) Pipe a second layer of cream,

leaving a little in the bag for decorating the top. Place the other disc of phyllo on top of the cream. Press down very gently to make a large cream sandwich. Brush with another ¼ cup of the syrup and decorate the top with the remaining mascarpone cream. Sprinkle with chopped pistachios and rose petals. To serve, use a serrated knife to cut the entire cake in half, then cut each half in half. Cut again to make 8 slices. Serve with the remaining 1 cup syrup on the side so each person can drizzle over their slice. Osmalieh is best eaten on the same day.

Edy's Tip: *Shredded phyllo is often found in the freezer aisle of big grocery stores. It's also found in Middle Eastern and Greek grocery stores and online.*

Floral Knafeh

My grandfather Afif and I would make a weekly journey to Hallab 1881, a famous pastry store in Tripoli. While I stuck to the savory side, he was there for one thing: knafeh, a Lebanese version of cheesecake. Traditionally it's made with semolina breadcrumbs, which are hard to come by. For years I made it with shredded phyllo instead. But more recently, a new generation of Lebanese cooks have been using crushed cornflakes, which is a perfect solution and easy to source. In the summer of 2022, I went back to Lebanon. My grandfather was sick in bed, but I kept our tradition alive and went to Tripoli, brought back his favorite treat, and fed it to him. This recipe is for him and the memories we've shared.

Makes 12 squares

Nonstick cooking spray

For the syrup:
1 cup sugar
¼ cup rosewater

For the knafeh:
4 quarts cornflakes
1 cup (2 sticks) unsalted butter, melted
1 pound mozzarella cheese, shredded
1 pound ricotta cheese
⅓ cup honey
2 tablespoons orange blossom water
2 tablespoons rosewater
1 teaspoon kosher salt
Chopped pistachios, for garnish

1. Preheat the oven to 400°F. Coat a 9 by 13-inch baking dish with nonstick spray.

2. Make the syrup: In a small saucepan, add 1 cup water with the sugar and rosewater. Set over medium heat, bring to a simmer, and cook for 15 minutes without stirring, until the sugar has dissolved and the mixture is a little syrupy. Remove from the heat and set aside to cool.

3. Make the knafeh: Place the cornflakes in a large bowl. Use your hands to lightly crush the flakes into uneven crumbs. Toss with the butter until fully coated.

4. In a separate medium bowl, stir the mozzarella cheese, ricotta cheese, honey, orange blossom water, rosewater, and salt until combined.

5. Press half of the crushed cornflakes into the bottom of the prepared baking dish, making an even base layer. Spread the cheese mixture over the top. Sprinkle the remaining cornflakes on top and press down to make an even layer. Bake for 25 to 30 minutes, until golden brown and bubbly. Spoon ½ cup of the syrup over the entire surface. Garnish with the pistachios. Cut into 12 squares and serve with the remaining syrup on the side. Knafeh is best enjoyed the same day.

Turkish Coffee Tiramisu

During my time in Italy, I made more tiramisu than I care to remember. It's my dad's favorite dessert, so in his honor I've swapped in Turkish coffee, the espresso of the Middle East. (Cold brew and espresso both work well here too.) But my special touch is adding crushed hazelnut biscotti to the cream for a great crunch and nutty flavor boost to this simple but perfect dessert.

1. Make the cream: In a stand mixer fitted with the whisk attachment (or a large bowl with an electric hand mixer), beat the egg yolks and sugar together until they triple in volume, about 5 minutes. Add the mascarpone and beat until combined. Transfer the mixture to a large bowl.

2. Wash and dry the mixer bowl, then return it to the stand mixer. Add the egg whites and beat to soft peaks, about 3 minutes. Gradually fold the egg whites and liqueur into the mascarpone mixture. Add the heavy cream to the mixer bowl (no need to clean it) and beat to soft peaks, about 3 minutes. Fold the whipped cream and half of the crushed biscotti into the mascarpone mixture.

3. To assemble, dust the bottom of a 9 by 13-inch baking dish with cocoa powder. Working one at a time, dip the ladyfingers into the Turkish coffee and arrange in the baking dish until you have an even layer. Spread half of the mascarpone mixture over the ladyfingers. Continue dipping while arranging a second layer of ladyfingers over the mascarpone. Spread the remaining mascarpone mixture over the top, then cover with plastic wrap and chill in the refrigerator for at least 4 hours (if you can wait 24 hours, all the better). Sprinkle the remaining crushed biscotti over the top before serving. Tiramisu can be covered and refrigerated for up to 3 days.

Serves 10 to 12

For the cream:

8 large eggs, whites and yolks separated

1 cup granulated sugar

1 pound mascarpone cheese, at room temperature

1 tablespoon orange liqueur, such as Grand Marnier (optional)

1½ cups heavy cream

6 ounces hazelnut biscotti, finely crushed

For assembly:

Cocoa powder

48 ladyfingers, from 2 (7-ounce) packages

1½ cups brewed Turkish coffee (page 87) or other strong brewed coffee, cooled

Edy's Tip: Assemble the tiramisu in disposable cups for perfect individual portions! Dip 1 or 2 ladyfingers in the coffee, then break into the bottom of the cup. Depending on the size of your cup, scoop a few spoonfuls of the cream to reach about halfway up. Repeat with another layer of ladyfingers and cream to top off the cup before chilling. Sprinkle the remaining crushed biscotti on top before serving.

Golden Sfouf

VG

Sfouf is a traditional Lebanese Easter cake, which I always looked forward to eating but never made until we were celebrating the Grocer's first Easter. Making the cake with semolina flour, a coarse-grained wheat, instead of all-purpose, gives it a nice bite. The pine nuts, almonds, and sesame on top add a decadent crunch, and the orange blossom syrup is a sweet and fragrant touch, but the bright yellow color from the turmeric is what really makes this an Easter delicacy. It's equally perfect for a special occasion or alongside tea in the morning.

Makes 12 pieces

3 tablespoons tahini (for greasing the dish)

For the syrup:
1 cup granulated sugar
½ cup orange blossom water

For the cake:
2 cups semolina flour
2 tablespoons ground turmeric
1 teaspoon kosher salt
1 teaspoon baking powder
1 cup granulated sugar
¾ cup extra-virgin olive oil
3 large eggs
1 cup plain fat-free Greek yogurt
2 tablespoons sesame seeds
2 tablespoons slivered almonds
2 tablespoons pine nuts

1. Preheat the oven to 325°F. Drizzle the tahini into a 9 by 13-inch baking dish and use clean hands to rub it all over to grease the dish.
2. Make the syrup: In a small saucepan, add 1 cup water with the sugar and orange blossom water. Set over medium heat, bring to a simmer, and cook for 15 minutes without stirring, until the sugar has dissolved and the mixture is a little syrupy. Set aside to cool.
3. Make the cake: In a medium bowl, whisk the semolina flour, turmeric, salt, and baking powder together.
4. In a stand mixer fitted with the whisk attachment (or a large bowl with an electric hand mixer), beat the sugar and olive oil together for about 2 minutes, until well combined. Add the eggs one at a time and continue beating for about 2 more minutes, until airy. Gradually spoon the flour mixture into the batter and beat until incorporated. Add the yogurt and mix until just combined.
5. Pour the batter into the prepared baking dish. In a small bowl, toss the sesame seeds, almonds, and pine nuts, then sprinkle the mixture over the cake. Bake for 25 to 30 minutes, rotating the baking dish halfway, until a toothpick inserted in the center comes out clean. Remove from the oven and cool in the baking dish for 10 minutes. Spoon ½ cup of the syrup over the entire surface of the cake. Cut the cake diagonally in 3 slices, then rotate the pan and cut 4 slices diagonally in the opposite direction to create diamonds. Serve immediately, with the remaining syrup on the side. Store, covered, at room temperature for up to 1 week.

Lemony Rosewater Cake

VG

My Teita Odette's signature dessert was an orange cake, which I never got the chance to learn from her before she left us. This modern lemon and rosewater version is my best imitation of my culinary role model's showstopper. I did a lot of recipe testing to get this just right, trying to conjure up how Odette might have baked it. After experimenting with different flours, I felt like semolina and almond flour were the best combo for a light, chewy, crumbly texture. Using olive oil, the butter of Lebanese baking, was an easy decision. Rosewater syrup added the delicate floral accent her cake had. And, of course, I had to add lemon to always keep it zesty. This recipe makes a 9-inch cake but can be divided between two 5 by 9-inch loaf pans or muffin tins to make 12 muffins.

1. Preheat the oven to 350°F. Coat a 9-inch cake pan or springform pan with nonstick spray.
2. Make the syrup: In a small saucepan, add 1 cup water with the sugar. Set over medium heat, bring to a simmer, and cook for 15 minutes without stirring, until the sugar has dissolved and the mixture is a little syrupy. Add the lemon slices and simmer for about 5 more minutes, until the slices have released their juice. Remove from the heat and add the rosewater. Set a fine-mesh strainer over a medium bowl. Strain the syrup into the bowl and set aside. Set the lemon slices on a wire rack to cool.
3. Make the cake: In a medium bowl, whisk the almond flour, semolina flour, salt, and baking powder together.
4. In a stand mixer fitted with the whisk attachment (or a large bowl with an electric hand mixer), beat the sugar and olive oil together for about 2 minutes, until combined. Add the eggs one at a time and continue beating for about 2 more minutes, until airy. Gradually spoon the flour mixture into the batter and beat until incorporated. Add the lemon juice and mix until just combined.
5. Pour the batter into the prepared cake pan. Bake for 40 to 45 minutes, rotating the pan halfway, until a toothpick inserted in the center comes out clean. Remove from the oven and spoon ½ cup of the syrup over the entire surface of the cake. Cool in the pan for 15 minutes.
6. Run a sharp knife or offset spatula around the edge of the cake. Set a serving plate over the cake pan, then flip the cake onto the plate. Arrange the reserved candied lemon slices over the top before serving, with the remaining syrup on the side. Store, covered, at room temperature for up to 3 days.

Serves 8

Nonstick cooking spray

For the syrup:
1 cup granulated sugar
1 lemon, thinly sliced
¼ cup rosewater

For the cake:
1 cup almond flour
1 cup semolina flour
1 teaspoon kosher salt
1 teaspoon baking powder
1 cup granulated sugar
¾ cup extra-virgin olive oil
3 large eggs
¼ cup fresh lemon juice

Edy's Tip: *This cake freezes very well! Wrap tightly in plastic wrap and freeze for up to 3 months. Thaw overnight in the refrigerator before serving.*

Fig & Sesame Ricotta Cake

VG, NF

I spent a summer working as a private chef in the Hamptons and basically made the same dessert all summer. This simple ricotta cake is so moist and the perfect canvas for any produce. I'm partial to figs, but that summer I followed the lead of what was in season, decorating my cakes with the ripest fruit from the farmers' market, such as peaches, apricots, plums, or berries. The finishing touch, a topping of brown sugar and sesame seeds, gets caramelized and crunchy in the oven for a perfectly balanced cake.

Serves 6 to 8

Nonstick cooking spray

½ cup (1 stick) unsalted butter

1 cup fig jam

1½ cups semolina flour

1 cup granulated sugar

2 teaspoons baking powder

1 teaspoon kosher salt

3 large eggs

8 ounces ricotta cheese (2 cups)

8 fresh figs, halved

2 tablespoons dark brown sugar

3 tablespoons sesame seeds

1. Preheat the oven to 350°F. Coat a 9-inch springform pan with nonstick spray.

2. In a small saucepan, melt the butter over medium heat and bring to a simmer. Continue simmering, and occasionally swirling the pan, until the butter foams, then starts to subside, and brown specks start to appear at the bottom. Cook until golden brown and nutty smelling, then remove from the heat and whisk in the fig jam. Set aside.

3. In a medium bowl, whisk the semolina flour, granulated sugar, baking powder, and salt together. Set aside.

4. In a stand mixer fitted with the whisk attachment (or a large bowl with an electric hand mixer), beat the eggs and ricotta together for about 2 minutes, until light and fluffy. Gradually spoon the flour mixture into the batter and beat until incorporated. Remove the bowl from the mixer and fold in the brown butter mixture.

5. Pour the batter into the prepared cake pan. Arrange the halved figs, cut side up, over the surface, then sprinkle the top of the cake with the brown sugar and sesame seeds. Bake for 50 to 55 minutes, rotating the pan every 15 minutes, until a toothpick inserted in the center comes out clean. Remove the springform and transfer the cake to a wire rack to cool before serving. Store, covered, at room temperature for up to 3 days.

Kesak

8

Refreshing
Drinks to
Get You
Through the
Night

Lemonade Chart

When life gives you lemons . . . you keep it zesty! And I couldn't call this book *Keep It Zesty* without including at least one lemonade. So, I included six! At the Grocer, we run a thriving lemonade stand out the coffee window all summer. It's sweet, refreshing, and an extremely popular choice for everyone who wants to beat the heat on their walks to McCarren Park. At home, I like to make a big batch and always keep a pitcher in my fridge. These are my favorite flavors—they can easily be mixed together, and all of them can be livened up with a splash of vodka.

Note: To make simple syrup, add 1 cup sugar and 1 cup water to a small saucepan over high heat. Bring to a boil, then lower the heat and simmer until the sugar is dissolved. Remove from the heat and cool completely, about 1 hour. You can make a larger batch using the 1:1 ratio and store in the refrigerator for up to 1 month.

The Mother Lemonade

V, GF, NF

Serves 6

4 cups cold water
1 cup simple syrup
2 cups fresh lemon juice

Add the ingredients to a blender. Blend on high speed for about 30 seconds, until fully combined. Pour into a pitcher and let the foam settle for 5 minutes. Serve in glasses filled with ice.

Cucumber Lemonade	Rosewater Lemonade	Minty Lemonade	Strawberry Lemonade	Blackberry Basil Lemonade
V, GF, NF	V, GF, NF	V, GF, NF	V, GF, NF	V, GF, NF
Blend with: 2 cucumbers, peeled, seeds removed, and roughly chopped	Blend with: ¾ cup rosewater	Blend with: ½ cup fresh mint leaves	Blend with: 8 ounces strawberries, fresh or frozen (about 2 cups)	Blend with: 6 ounces blackberries, fresh or frozen (about 1½ cups) ¾ cup fresh basil leaves

Edy's Tip: *Make it a party by adding 2 cups vodka, tequila, or gin to any of these lemonades!*

Minty Watermelon Surfer

(V, GF, NF)

I made this watermelon drink for my first-ever pop-up in New York, a Taiwanese-Lebanese brunch with my friend and fellow food-lover Leiti Hsu. I served it directly out of the watermelon with edible flowers floating on the surface. (The beachy vibes of the drink and the bobbing flowers reminded me of surfers.) It was a hit, so I kept making it for events until it became a signature drink. There's nothing more refreshing than watermelon juice on a hot New York evening—so cooling and naturally sweet—and the lime juice and mint make for a perfect trio.

Serves 6

1 small seedless watermelon (about 3½ pounds)
½ cup fresh lime juice (about 4 limes)
⅓ cup fresh mint leaves
1 cup cold water

Cut the watermelon into large pieces and trim away the rind. Add the watermelon to a blender with the lime juice, mint leaves, and water. Start on low and increase the speed to high until the ingredients are fully blended, about 2 minutes. Pour into a small pitcher and let sit for about 20 minutes, until the foam dissipates. Serve in glasses filled with ice.

Edy's Tip: *Slice ¼ inch from each end of the watermelon to make a flat base, then cut the watermelon in half. Use a large spoon to scoop out the watermelon flesh from both halves. Use one scooped-out half as a punch bowl by setting it on a large serving platter with a ladle, and pour the finished drink in it. If you like, add 1½ cups gin, vodka, or tequila for a real party!*

Pomegranate Moscow Mule

V, GF, NF

When my best friend, Mila, and I left culinary school and moved to New York, we drank Moscow mules everywhere we went. We were underage and excited to be out in the city, plus Moscow mules were having a moment back then—you could spot those copper mugs at every bar in Brooklyn! We've grown up and switched to martinis now, but I still have a soft spot for a mule. My own version adds pomegranate juice and seeds for a tart and festive touch, especially around Christmas when I make this the most.

Add the vodka, pomegranate juice, simple syrup, lime juice, and ginger beer to a small pitcher. Stir well to combine. Pour into individual rocks glasses filled with ice. Garnish with pomegranate seeds, a rosemary sprig, and a lime wedge.

Serves 4

1 cup vodka

1 cup pomegranate juice

¼ cup simple syrup (see note, page 230)

¼ cup fresh lime juice

18 ounces ginger beer

Pomegranate seeds, rosemary sprigs, and lime wedges, for serving

Edy's Tip: *For a smoky drink, use a match to light a small rosemary sprig on fire. Blow out the flame, place the sprig on a cutting board, and set the glass on top. Let the lingering smoke fill the glass while you assemble the cocktail.*

Jallab Rosey Iced Tea

V, GF

Jallab, a fruit syrup popular in the Middle East, is the basis of this drink, which we used to get from street vendors in Tripoli. Jallab is hard to come by in the US, but I found that a mix of date molasses and rosewater is pretty close in flavor. The most luxurious part of the drink is the raw pine nuts on top, something rich and flavorful to chew on with each sip. A splash of vodka wouldn't be out of place either!

Serves 6

4 cups cold water
¾ cup date molasses
½ cup rosewater
Pine nuts, to garnish

Add the water, date molasses, and rosewater to a blender. Blend for about 1 minute, until the molasses is fully incorporated. Serve in glasses filled with ice and top with a sprinkle of pine nuts.

Spicy Sumac Margarita

V, GF, NF

Who doesn't love a margarita? It's such a classic cocktail, perfect for events and hosting at home. I like to make big batches for a party or my Shawarma Chicken Taco Night (page 166) and put it in bottles so everyone can serve themselves. I know it might seem like a lot of limes to squeeze, but the fresh juice is worth it and it's an easy project to tackle a day or two in advance. The rim here is a mix of flaky salt for crunch and Aleppo pepper for a spicy kick. The tequila helps cool the heat, while the sumac enhances the tangy lime flavor for a tingly, flavorful drink.

Add the lime juice, tequila, simple syrup, and sumac to a small pitcher and whisk until well combined and a little frothy, about 2 minutes. Spoon 3 tablespoons of the margarita mix from the pitcher onto a small dish. On a separate small dish, add the flaky salt and Aleppo pepper. Use the back of a soup spoon to crush and combine until the mixture is pale red. Dip each glass into the margarita mixture, then the salt mixture. Fill with ice and pour over the margarita. Garnish with a lime wedge. Kesak!

Serves 6

3 cups fresh lime juice (14 to 16 limes)

2 cups silver tequila

1 cup simple syrup (see note, page 230)

2 tablespoons sumac

2 tablespoons flaky sea salt

2 tablespoons Aleppo pepper

Lime wedges, for serving

Rosewater Spritz

V, GF, NF

Like a good New York gay, my drink of choice is a vodka soda. This rosewater-spiked version is so light and refreshing. There's no sweetener, but the rosewater flavor gives the idea of sweetness and somehow masks the vodka taste. It goes down easy (maybe a little too easy) like a cold seltzer on a hot afternoon.

Add the vodka, rosewater, and lemon juice to a small pitcher and stir to combine. Add the sparkling water and gently stir three times to combine. Serve in glasses filled with ice and garnish with a lemon wheel or rose petals.

Serves 4

1½ cups vodka

½ cup rosewater

¼ cup fresh lemon juice

1 liter sparkling water, such as San Pellegrino or Topo Chico

Lemon wheels or dried rose petals, for serving

Edy's Tip: *Make sure to source edible dried flowers, usually found in spice shops or easily bought online.*

Arak Dirty Martini

V, GF, NF

We're currently in the middle of a martini renaissance, and I'm loving it! But when a drink is so classic, it's hard to find a way to reinvent it. One day, while digging through my liquor cabinet, I realized the answer was right in front of me. Arak—a Lebanese anise liquor. It starts clear and turns cloudy when mixed with water, so by the time it hits the glass it'll be opaque and creamy. If you can't find arak, ouzo (its Greek counterpart) is a great substitute, but it's worth the effort to get the real thing. Just a warning: arak is very high in alcohol, so sip with caution.

Makes 1 martini

Fill a cocktail shaker with ice. Add the arak, vermouth, olive juice, and water. Shake well and strain into a martini glass. Garnish with olives.

2 ounces arak
1 ounce dry vermouth
½ ounce olive juice
2 ounces cold water
Olives, for garnish

Note: If arak is too strong for your taste, use a ratio of 1 ounce arak, 1 ounce vodka, and 1 ounce vermouth.

Make this in batches (just multiply by how many you need to serve) and refrigerate in glass bottles until it's time to serve. Set up a martini bar and let everyone pour their own.

Edy's Tip

Acknowledgments

I have purchased and flipped through hundreds of cookbooks in my life, but writing one changes the way you look at the whole experience. So much time and effort goes into every page, every word, every crumb in each picture. Without my amazing team, family, friends, and our Greenpoint community, this book wouldn't have been born!

To my parents, Paola and Simon, I am always so grateful for the way you raised us around food and made it part of our life. Thank you for being brave and moving to the US, because without your decision I wouldn't have been able to make an impact in Brooklyn.

To my sister, Natacha, thank you for reading over every agreement and contract, and being my number one motivator throughout this journey. My story wouldn't be complete without you by my side through every step.

To my aunt Dina, these recipes exist because you keep Teita's traditions alive through your cooking. Thank you for your expertise and for keeping me well fed every time I come to Lebanon.

To the Raffais, from the moment we met in the elevator of the CIA to now, you have been my family. Guylene, thank you for testing every recipe for me and being so precise about every step. Sophia, thank you for being a great cheerleader and tasting every dish! Mila, my rock, thank you for helping me develop, write, test, and test again every recipe and for running the Grocer while I was far away in my writing cave! Thank you is never enough for the Raffais.

To Jack, thank you for being an amazing partner throughout every project I have taken. Thank you for tasting each recipe over and over again and listening to me complain about the lows and the highs. Love you.

To my amazing lemony Grocer team, without you our pink and green corner would not be the same. I am so proud to call you family—you bring the zest to Greenpoint and make me proud of what we have built together every day.

To Isabella Xia, the visionary behind our brand, you make us shine with all your beautiful graphics and illustrations. You bring so much light and positivity into the Grocer every day. Our social media wouldn't be the same without you behind the camera, making me laugh and splicing up my bloopers. Thank you for always bringing my vision to life.

To Casey Elsass, thank you for bringing my words to paper. Planning and working on this book together has been a dream of mine come to life. Your expertise and precise editing made this such an enjoyable process.

To my photographer, Jessica Marx, and prop stylist, Julia Rose: boxed into six hundred square feet, we were able to make magic happen. Thank you for being the most amazing team I could have ever asked for to shoot and bring my recipes to life. Eight days of making absolute magic, no matter the hurdles, we got through it because, let's never forget, less is more!!

To my editor, Ezra Kupor, you were a follower from day one and you believed in the Keep It Zesty vision before I even believed it myself. Thank you for making a home for this book and fighting for my vision every step of the way. And to Bonni Leon-Berman and the entire team at HarperCollins, thank you for making my dream a reality.

To Nicole Tourtelot and Nora Gonzalez, thank you for believing in this book from start to finish. I couldn't have done it without your support!

To Karly Stillman, you've been there through it all, baby, and here's to the next chapter. From seeing Oprah at the Barclays Center, to pushing me to do more and advance with every step, I don't know what this journey would have been like without you. Now let's get on the road.

To my friends: Grossy, Jamesy, Sam, Afif, Alison, Keryn, Sophie, Allie, William, Kelsie, and many more, thank you for answering my texts and calls and testing, tasting, and supporting this zesty journey.

To Hay, EQ3, good neighbor, Felt+Fat, Alex Mill, and Bed Threads, thank you for providing us with amazing props to make our whimsical poppy vision shine.

Index

(Page references in *italics* refer to illustrations.)

About the Author

Born in Lebanon, Edy Massih trained at the Culinary Institute of America and began as a Brooklyn-based private chef and caterer before opening Edy's Grocer, a Lebanese market and restaurant in Greenpoint, Brooklyn. The Grocer was an immediate hit and Edy was named a Forbes 30 Under 30 of Food and Drink in 2022. Inspired by the flavors and colors of the Middle East, Edy's unique take on Mediterranean cuisine stems from the recipes he grew up perfecting in the kitchen with his grandmothers.

HarperCollins books may be purchased for educational,
business, or sales promotional use. For information, please email
the Special Markets Department at SPsales@harpercollins.com.

FIRST EDITION

Designed by Bonni Leon-Berman
Illustrations by Isabella Xia
Photography by Jessica Marx
Food styling by Edy Massih and Mila Raffai
Prop styling by Julia Rose
Cover food styling by Greg Lofts
Personal photographs from Edy's archive and Kelsey Cherry
Photographs in Lebanon by Michele Aoun

Library of Congress Cataloging-in-Publication Data has been
applied for.

ISBN 978-0-06-328090-8

24 25 26 27 28 TC 10 9 8 7 6 5 4 3 2 1